POLYSEMY

Marvin Bram

Copyright 2014 Marvin Bram

POLYSEMY

Polysemy

My memory, which I hope I'm not embellishing, is that we in the audience could see the agitated dust in the beams cast by the spotlights behind us. That there were two extraordinary people standing on the small stage of the old, uncomfortable auditorium is certain. What one of these people was about to show us would persuade me that I was levitating.

The young woman on the stage was a deaf poet. She was accompanied by a cheerful, elderly man who had been talking to us about ASL, American Sign Language, for almost an hour. His aim was to teach us a reasonable number of signs, with particular attention to signs made by one hand rather than two. Most of us had been moving our own hands, imitating him, smiling at his anecdotes, and wondering what the poet was eventually going to do. He was molding us, I think, into a state of receptivity to her intentions.

ASL isn't just another language; it's another kind of language. French is another language; Sanskrit is another language. Middle Egyptian is another kind of language. ASL is unlike French and Sanskrit, and like Middle Egyptian. It's only since 1960 that the academic community has acknowledged that ASL is a language at all. Its users have always known that it's a language, but their teachers had often regarded it as merely something vaguely like a language. Because ASL was incomplete, teachers would argue, or unsatisfactory on some other ground, it wasn't worth teaching. That changed, and now you can take ASL as a second language in many colleges and universities. That doesn't mean that we're to think of ASL as just another second language, of course. It's more than that.

I studied the Middle Egyptian writing system, which silently communicates on funerary walls what ASL silently communicates in the space between its signers, at the Oriental Institute at the University of Chicago. Once, bent over a papyrus, my teacher quietly said that any one hieroglyph can be a poem. I asked him whether such hieroglyphs were found in what we would ordinarily call a poem, a piece composed on a distinctive, poetic subject, juxtaposing words in unique ways, and attending to Egyptian equivalents of line lengths and rhythms. He turned to me and said that a hieroglyph in a laundry list can be a poem, and the laundry list can be a poem with the weight of an entire poetic literature.

Then what *is* a poem? For my teacher a poem didn't have to be the sort of object I'd asked him about. Many poems since the effective end of the Egyptian writing system 3500 years ago have indeed been such objects; we post-1500 BC readers have got used to calling them poems, and we value many of them. We admire their subjects, their original juxtapositions of words, their rhythms. We're moved by striking metaphors and similes. Leaving what for one-word poems? Polysemy.

A polysemy is a multi-referential object that directs meanings at you as long as you contemplate it. It is storied, and the stories are of indefinite length. It feeds your psyche the way the food that best nourishes you feeds your body. The psychoanalyst Christopher Bollas calls objects that (a) we need to experience, (b) are associated with reverie as the mode of experiencing them, (c) make us happy when they're present, and (d) make us sad when they're not present, "evocative objects." Polysemies are evocative objects. It's appropriate to call polysemous Egyptian hieroglyphs "objects," since many of the incised or drawn two-dimensional signs we're familiar with were three-dimensional, carved totems first.

A single ASL sign, gestured in time, more an event than an object, can be as much a polysemy as a multi-referential Egyptian hieroglyph frozen on a tomb wall for millennia. One summer I spent a week at a signing camp for hearing adults in Canada. My fellow students and I were without doubt happy when we were signing, clumsy as we were, and sad when we weren't.

We found that we needed to sign. Was that because signing was nutritious in some way, and strongly evocative? Was the everyday state-of-mind of that summer one of reverie? Gaston Bachelard is a champion of reverie. Reverie is the stance of consciousness that adds dreamwork to wakefulness, and that Bachelard says gets us to the "bottom" of signs, as if signs were wells the depths of which aren't accessible to wakefulness by itself. Canada seemed decisively to confirm the kinship of Middle Egyptian and ASL.

Back to the dusty auditorium. If one ASL sign can be a poem defined as a polysemy, then what are two different one-handed ASL signs received together? The young deaf poet answered that question in her performance. She signed a poem with one hand and a different poem with the other hand; what we experienced was the product of the two poems, polysemy to the second power. I was speechless with elation, first because of the excess of feeling while receiving her dialectical poetry, and later because I couldn't think how to describe so unprecedented an elation. I resolved to attempt approximations of her more-than-doubled polysemy using our less-than-polysemous English lexicon.

Please read each of the following yoked pairs of lines as if it were a single line, in the way you might puzzle out the treble and bass lines of a piano score separately, and then play them together. Please "play" the doublets. They make up an early teaching piece for a group of fifteen- and sixteen-year-olds who went on to compose reams of doublets themselves.

Singsong

Inside   out.
Humpback whales

Topsy   turvy;
Play and wander,

Have some pie.
Singing   fugues.

Say   too   much,
Such poor words,

Make up words;
Busy   plans;

Don't ask   why.
Think what's lost.

Kindly   jokes;
Use your hands.

To smile, to live,
So much to tell,

To laugh, to   give.
The sea knows well.

. . .

Hum   and   whistle.
Humpbacks singing:

Both at once.
Once is twice.

To keep the two strands of each doublet lined up for simultaneous reading, I tried to match the numbers of syllables in each strand. That's why the strands are laid out on the page the way they are. When they weren't writing equisyllabic doublets themselves, the students experimented with speaking doublets aloud, one speaker on each strand, stretching and compressing the times it took to align the spoken syllables and arrive at the end of each doublet together. Essentially, though, the point was to read, to play, the doublets silently, allowing two words at a time their entry into the reader's mind. Some of the simultaneous entries, we hoped, would invite a reader down into the pair, to stop, before continuing slowly to the right.

This was for the students' teachers.

Identity

It has been hard fully   to understand
Welcome to   the basement. This will be fun.

That   I   am a   separate   person
Could there be a sub-basement as well?

With   an   interior   known only to me,
Does light reach either of these buried places?

Only parts of which I am able to   reveal.
We have a   gallery   of mysteries down here.

Polysemy

I have a faint   memory of not knowing much of this.
Listen to me. Our mother isn't   alive   any more .

But   now   I understand more and more
She's dead. Can we become our   mother?

Of my interior   life, and   I make   better judgments   generally.
Very difficult. "Become," I said. Does that mean that you and I are

 I   am more responsive to motives   I   finally see,
Less than one self or one self or two selves? Definitely

 About   what to   make known
Too hard. Too hard right   now.

And what to conceal.
Time to   be quiet.

My   interior   is clay   I can work.
Stop turning over up there. Go to sleep.

. . .

Time must be shaped as well.
Here we are: Aesthetics.

 I know the shape of my past,
Look back and you see patterns.

 Especially of   its imperfections,
Martyrdom. It's purple melodrama.

From which   I hope I have learned.
Now   it's…whoa… Pedagogy.

Polysemy

The future will have the shape
You, camper, will love this camp.

That will complete the shape
Let the burden slip, please.

My past *ought* to have had.
What do you know of this?

Inside the pattern from my birth to death.
The past? A pattern? Accidents. Relax.

I will give form to each decade,
Do you think time is clay to work?

To each year, each month, week, and day.
Do you think our mind, yours and mine,

Each will have a beginning, middle, and end.
Depends on this beginning, middle, and end

Each short-run beginning, middle, and end
Business? Sounds like school essays to me.

Will be part of a next-longer-run beginning
Good essays, of course. Paragraphs in good order,

And middle and end.
Conclusions sewn up,

The same will be true of each still-longer run
Each small part nested inside a larger part.

In the single whole of my   life.
The somber method of the schools.

Good shape in   my inner life;
  But   you must be joking: life,

Good shape over my life's whole span,
Death, an   iron   logic   in   time?

The   orderliness   of my days, weeks, and years
You need not go on in this   heavy,   sad way.

Assured   as much as I can assure   it.
"Assured." Better to eat a buttered roll.

   I   can face death with courage.
Death can take care   of   itself.

    . . .

Then how *will* I   face death?
Who   is   this "I" you mean?

What do you mean?
Were we born "I?"

"I"   learned that   I am a   separate   person.
You learned that, exactly as you said before.

Am   I   to unlearn my separateness?
You went on to learn   differentiation

What would I have remaining to me
  In   every   act, dividing up

Polysemy

Were I to lose my difference?
Each part into still smaller parts.

I might have or be nothing.
At the end, you have nothing.

Yet…perhaps there is something to learn,
Stop it. We don't want gloom anymore.

Not simply something to unlearn and dispense with.
No more "time." Begin to turn your thoughts on their heads.

If I do not differentiate one thing from another,
What you used to differentiate, one thing from another,

Must I *de*differentiate?
Let's now dedifferentiate.

If I do not claim difference,
No longer "this differs from that,"

Must I claim identity?
But "this is – the strong 'is' – that."

I would be myself and this other thing, too,
Stronger, more cheerful. When a child does such things,

Animate or inanimate –
She wants to laugh, a clear, strong sign

Other things, plural, all simultaneously.
Of health, rather than the frowns crowning distinctions.

As   I neared death
It's right to   laugh,

I would near becoming   every   thing.
To make less sense, to forget most things.

Before returning to   the earth,
Become a turtle, stone, chair, salt,

 I would become   the earth.
This friend, that kid, the earth.

Before joining my mother in death,
To be   happy follows: enlargement,

 I would   become my mother in life.
Laughter. To be kind follows: never

The   I who perished
Hurt, the   only rule.

Would be   a small part of   the large   I   I'd become.
 Born one thing, die   all things – the mind's right and power,

The rest persists.
To grow, to sing.

This is the opening page of the second movement of J.S. Bach's Third Unaccompanied Sonata for violin, "Fuga." It will give us a musical "line of variable depth." We'll look for whether a verbal line of variable depth can yield with words, for a reader, what Bach's musical line yields with tones, for a listener.

These passages begin one of the longest and most perfect fugues Bach wrote. But the violin can't sound a fugue the way a keyboard instrument can. The thickest texture available to the violinist is a doubling, two strings bowed at the same time. But Bach picked the violin for this fugue, as if a special majesty would attach to drawing polyphony from a small wooden box with four strings stretched across it.

The Fugue moves in at least four modes: (1) strict singularity, one note after another, (2) generative singularity, one note after another implying counterpoint, (3) strict doubling, two lines sounding together, and (4) generative doubling, two lines sounding together implying one, two, and even three additional, unsounded but experienced lines – Bach's mightiest achievement, placing him uniquely in the history of Western consciousness.

Listen to the Fugue on a CD or on the Internet, perhaps four times. On the third listening, follow Bach's score for the first minutes at least. If you haven't followed scores before, simply progress left to right at the rate indicated by the half- quarter- eighth- and sixteenth-notes in the score, moving faster the shorter the note. As the notes rise up in the score, you'll hear them as higher pitches. Linking your eye to your ear will help you concentrate. Invite the generated, unsounded notes and phrases into consciousness; in time, they come.

Polyphony to polysemy. A polysemy like and unlike that of Middle Egyptian and ASL, modeled on Bach's fugues for solo violin, might be described this way: we have polysemy as a generative counterpoint of the meanings of English words written to be received simultaneously by a reader. Remaining with composers, the following piece was inspired by Bach's greatest reader:

Brahms

"A" is the mothernote.

I'll tell you where it is in a minute.

And what is the motherpulse?
  Seventy-two, the heartbeat.

Now here is a question: what is the mother*piece?*

So: my mother, now dead,
A   kind of quiz. By Brahms;

Understood nothing of modern times.
 For violin   but not for   violin –

  I   would complain to her
This   is   related   to

  About   some complicated modern thing,
Where the mothernote can always be found –

Something she couldn't   possibly   understand,
  Because   we   need it; and now we can have it:

  And   she would look at me – excuse me for repeating –
Brahms's first   sonata   for   violin and piano

                       No need to speak.
  Look at me, in a way that defeats language,
Played lower,   on the   viola.
                       The mother's voice.

Polysemy

And the thing was no longer a question to be answered.
  This is our motherpiece, the music of origins.

 I wrote once about Norman's mother.
To return to our mothernote search.

She roamed the apartment late at night, asleep,
The sonata's opening settles on that "A,"

Checking on the children.
Your and my mothernote.

She was asleep.
How could she see?

Regarding such stories, collections of them
Go to an established violin dealer.

Will sometimes be prefaced
Look like you have money.

With their first letter, perhaps the letter "A."
(Don't worry; there's not a chance they will read this.)

The longest American poem is called "A,"
Look like a connoisseur of exquisite

Its first letter and line, "A."
Objects of every kind.

The entire collection or poem may be said to be contained in "A."
Ask somebody there to show you a great eighteenth-century viola.

Polysemy

The note "A" on the viola will sound all notes.
"Please play the opening measures of the Brahms,

The letter and the note are polysemies.
But if you don't mind, play them transcribed down."

The quest for polysemies:
"Hmm," say, as if pondering,

From single meanings to multiple meanings.
While acting calm, having heard the mothernote.

Mothertalk is multiple-meaning talk, not nonsense, but real sense.
Decide then what the best thing to do for you and the world might be.

School- science- business- and wartalk
　　The　　twenty-first　　　century

Are single-meaning talk, nonsense.
Need not be apocalyptic.

Each one of these forms injured my mother
Play the viola and work hard for life.

But she overcame all of them
Each is simple, each is complex.

　For my father, brother, me, and her memories of peace.
"Here's to a century of the viola and world peace."

　She had a hard time crossing streets.
Sounds like a naïve sentiment?

She never got the difference between stop and go signs.
Oh well, where has sophistication got us, anyway?

Nothing was always true for her.
Certainties are air: Roscelin.

If the sun were shining,
But music is substance,

But I, at eight, wanted to skip school…"snow!"
Free of impressive capitalized nouns.

We visited a violin maker who could hear the music in wood.
Our ancestors made mother figures of earth and stone everywhere;

I asked him why some people responded to the viola so warmly.
But the juggernaut in sight, they needed to hear her before night fell.

I asked the question, but he looked at my mother.
So they turned to wood, the ancient shape, and the fifth.

"Because it's the voice of the mother,
They carved a hollow mother figure

The mother who must die and the mother who will never die."
That gives us the song that roots our sleep and death in calm and life.

Reading different texts written to be read together doesn't have much of a history, but listening to different texts written to be sung together has a fascinating history. The great moment in the West is the twelfth to the fifteenth centuries, the era of polytextual motets. This is an early fifteenth-century Latin motet by John Dunstable. It tells the story of John the Baptist.

Preco preheminencio principi precessit, salus sapiencie subito successit; preco penitenciam prius
Precursor premittitur populum parare, nebulosis nittitur nova nunciare; deitatem

predicavit, princeps perpotenciam peccata purgavit; legislator latuit languidis largitus, precursor
domuit desenti decenter; perdicando profuit pluribus prudenter;

patuit prudens et peritus; limpha lavit liquada lubrica lugentem, turba tincta turbida timet et
carceris custodia captus coartatur; timens tantus

tingentem; missus ministerium magni mandatoris mutat in misterium modi melioris: Pax paterna
talia tyrannus turbatur. Crudeti convivio

panditur plebi penitenti, filius dum funditur flumine fluenti, descendit divinitus donum deitatis
caro convocavit, saltantem salario sacro saciavit

particeps paraclitus, princeps pietatis: singulare sequitur signum sanctitatis, tribus histribuitur
pars prima prescinditur proceris proceri, miseranda mittitur merces

tronus trinitatis. Cessit circumcisio, cella cecitatis, renovat renacio requiem renatis; premebatur
mulieri. Prestent per presidium preces

patria primitus penalis, renatos regia recipit regalis.
Precursoris sequentes subsidium sancti salvatoris.

Reception of double lines of text is more difficult when the texts are sung than when they're read. You can read as slowly as you wish, after all, and you can go back, read the top lines, then the bottom lines, and only then both lines at once. It's hard to imagine the magnitude of the motet-composers' expectations of their listeners.

Polysemy

In later centuries, opera librettists periodically set different texts to be sung at once. *Don Giovanni* begins that way and *The Marriage of Figaro* ends that way. Now and then a stage musical or a movie will put two popular songs together. Louis Zukofsky's poem "A" ends with a long contrapuntal episode that Celia Zukofsky composed using existing work by her husband. I know of no poetry through-written contrapuntally.

ON THE NATURE OF THINGS

Introduction

I

Why do I adopt a form like this,

I ask myself. The epics I regret

Are done in iambs and the other meters

So they'll march along like phalanx

Hoplites – brothers, selflessly coordinated

For killing children like themselves.

Since it's the content I object to, not so much

The form, let me change the martial posture

Homer and his imitators strike.

Such rhythm as supports my argument

Is borrowed not from battlefields but dancefloors,

Pulsing along cheerfully, let's say,

To something like, "The Promised Kiss of Springtime."

Then, perhaps, a dancelike form might carry

New accounts of human matters, less concerned

With heroes, striving, death, and glory,

And we can both proceed, you and I,

To move about the floor a while

To musics both the same and new.

II

All our distant kin are gone.

People like them recently, a few

Of them, at least, could talk to us,

But they are mostly gone as well.

So we are free to think they never lived,

Or if they did, they lived diminished lives.

We think this to our grievous loss.

I will call the time between

A quarter million years ago

And just five thousand years ago

The kinship era.

Can anything be said of it?

Yes, but not, I think, in single lines like these.

The mind of kinship's aegis differs from such minds

As yours and mine – however smart we think ourselves to be –

Even though regarding central nervous systems,

Theirs and ours, we are the same.

For their more ample minds we need a line

That's two strands deep, like dancers

Holding to each other, or like the scores

Of keyboard pieces –

Of say, "The Promised Kiss of Springtime."

One reads and plays such lines together;

Isn't that the case?

You may now guess that at the end of kinship's sway,

The change of mental life from theirs to ours

Resulted in depletion: from so-to-speak two strands per line

To one: from amplitude to bare report.

(Is it to our diminished powers that we owe

The condescension paid to older ways?)

III

In   order   to express our   deepest feelings
My kin and I become the   river   otter.

We sing and dance the stories
I   am made of   otter fur

Of our origins,   not in what
And human skin. The otter's

Would later be assumed to   be
Story   belongs to   me and

A distant past, not in time at all –
It belongs to   everyone in the

Out of time. They live elsewhere,
Otter clan.   I   always   keep

And because we sing, they live in us.
The   otter   totem   safe and at hand.

We   love to   be with kids, the old;
I'm sometimes mad at someone else,

We love to laugh and sleep.
My sister, my   uncle,

Anger is not unknown to us
But I'd never push or hit a

But we never hit another person.
Person, never. I am that person.

We want nothing to change.
My life   is   one thick day.

IV

The city came.

The boys who'd always sung

The way the elders did went off

To find another village site.

They then forgot the ways of home.

The river's edge grew large supplies

Of wheat, and if they dug

Spaced rivulets, the quantity

Exploded. All they had to do

Was say that earth was not to be

The many things she'd always been,

But only dirt.

No: earth was only dirt, important dirt,

Because the wheat came up,

But dirt. No thing was now to mean a host of things,

Polysemy

I am I, not an otter too.

I'm not my sister and myself.

She and I are different people,

So if I wish, I can injure her:

No hurt will come to me.

It used to be, when life was one thick day,

When all the time there was

Was that repeated day,

The world came into being

When I was born

And ended when I died.

But now? Time's a curse.

Infinite ticks before my birth;

Infinite ticks now follow death.

My life, now thin, a moment.

The ticks-before called history,

Packed with causes and effects,

The after-ticks the future,

Replete with plans and fantasies.

My life hung out between them,

Hankering for this and that.

A wall between my inner world and yours

Now lets me injure you.

It lets me sell to you –

How nice for me.

We use each other

Without regret.

Each of us will try to leave a mark

On a future quite oblivious

To our lamenting cries.

Or we can try recovery,

As from a recent illness,

Recovering our ancient ways

Cosmogony

At the first   moment when   it could be said
In the first, shapeless space, free of light and

 That something had happened,
Sound and thought of   itself,

Two of the myriad pieces moved together,
Two of the myriad pieces moved together,

Joined, and became a larger piece.
Joined, and began the ruling fugue.

 Before that moment, the pieces had hovered
Stillness was complete before the first movement

Motionless,   each some distance from the rest.
Resounded through the   elder   space, to forge

No one knows quite why
     Original   time,

 This first movement occurred,
Twice sung, fugal,   stronger

 Or why it   resulted in a joining
Than our time, vertical, not causal;

  Rather   than   a circling or wandering.
And more than deep, too, a kairos, made of

 It is by no means certain either
All possible   energies compacted.

What the pieces were, exactly;
 All this begun by conjunction.

They may just have been condensations
The moment   before   original time,

Of the stuff   in between them,
The unknown world, before our

Thick enough   to have   surfaces.
World, neither possessed properties

But they may not have been that at all,
Nor did   not possess   properties; nor

Since each piece was in one   way or another
 Did   it stand   to our own world as potential

Polysemy

So different from each other piece,
To actual. Ways of being "there"

And their being condensations of one stuff
And "then" remain unreachable by us, bound

Would be hard to understand
   By our eyes and fingertips,

Unless the stuff varied considerably
Logics and glands, causal temporality,

From place to place.
Depth, length, and breadth.

Ever since that moment

The universe has been getting smaller and more dense.

  It appears that there is a tendency in the joinings
The moment that the new, causal time emerged, succession

Toward a center,
Joined conjunction.

So there would be a single outer surface
But as space drew in toward its new center,

Where there was none before:
Time thickened once again,

Now the universe boasts dimensions.
 In free counterpoint, raised to powers

Tomorrow there will be less outer surface,
  Ready to overwhelm   our local complaints,

 And   fewer   but more complicated,
Time complex and vast, reinstated.

More unlikely pieces inside   it.
The mystery of words is the same.

Large   pieces never   break into smaller ones.
All words contained words. Inside all written words

They accrete small   pieces,
Lived secret words, sheltered.

Or join to make larger pieces,
We can call them   into the light.

Or converge,   several   large pieces at a time,
The sentence like the word held interior sentences;

 To make extremely large pieces.
They too can emerge to   vision.

This last happens less   often than the simple joinings,
 At   last, after words and sentences are understood

Which are common.
   To   be   gravid,

Accretions are now
They are permitted

 The most common motions.
Their   natural   course, to

At different thresholds of size,
Bring new life. Then time itself,

The enlarging pieces acquire new properties.
Newly apprehended, reveals new properties:

All pieces, including the smallest, continue to move;
In all time other times lie in readiness for new life.

That is how it   all   started.
 The fugal rule: More from less.

 The larger the piece is,
(Spaces between the lines

The less movement it is capable of.
Are never as empty as they may look.)

Purpose is not   a   property,
Augmentation can be governed

But reflection is.
By reflection on

This is   to say that pieces   do not pick
Its ends. To say that increase is a good

Directions in   which to move;
Implicates ends: good for whom?

When they find
Good for life?

They have accreted onto another piece,
One may amplify any process or thing

  Or another piece has accreted onto them,
Which amplified serves life without irony.

  Or that they have been party to a joining
And one may make less of what subtracts from life.

Of some magnitude,
The rule protected:

They acquire increased awareness
 The increase of life, not of death.

Of the shape and nature of the larger piece
So   imagination   is itself enlarged.

They are part of.
  To imagine,

They acquire the same increase of awareness
  To create other pieces of other wholes,

Of pieces separate from them,
 Entirely other histories,

Both small and large.
Both less and more

Pieces larger than a piece in question
Layered than our everyday history,

Will stand as somewhat mysterious to it,
Becomes our fragile preeminent duty,

Polysemy

The more mystery,
The more difficult,

The greater the difference in size.
The greater the urgency, so large

No matter:
Are the stakes.

The piece in question will catch up,
The word well imagined   yields up

Since it will   inevitably   grow
 A healing alchemical heat. So

And will, in the end,
Too will the sentence,

Converge with the last other piece,
Dissolved   into   its   elements.

 Or be converged on.
Time no less than words

Since all the pieces were different
 Will, by   imaginings of music

From each other to begin with,
 In which nothing is excluded,

Each larger piece displays more internal difference
 Melodies   read as harmonies, become counterpoint

And more difference from   other   pieces.
      Uninterrupted,   transformed and ringing.

Reflection,
 Origins

The second property in   the order   of properties,
Imagined: beginnings in which orders of different

 And   the one that increases with each joining –
Kinds are created, re-making with each musing

  Motion   decreasing with each –
The world's   history   and end.

Is mainly admiration
To begin, admiration,

Of internal and external difference.
In attentive and lyrical   repeating:

   Reflection   is not expressed,
More from less, in the   kinship

There being no point to demonstrate
  Of action and word;   imaginings

Or   any   person   to persuade.
Of word or sentence,   origin,

   Reflection simply occurs, like motion.
Time, and life itself, granted, tended, sung.

There is a third property,
  From origins come forces

Polysemy

Only recently constituted a property,
Never afterward duplicated except by mind,

That bears some similarity to admiration,
 Little known to your and my everyday intercourse.

And might be called celebration.
 But imagined, remythicized,

When movement is sufficiently slowed
 The primary incandescent fact

And reflection sufficiently augmented,
Appears at the end and the beginning.

The next joining will be celebrated.
The next joining will be celebrated.

At those times, some pieces,
We turn to beginnings.

Likely to be quite large and stationary,
Look forward to the past, not to the future.

Various and reflective,
Looking to the future,

Will communicate with other pieces,
 Or rather, positing a true future,

Which will reciprocate admiration.
 Presents us with troubles represented

Smaller pieces often
   As   opportunities.

Reciprocate   with some intensity,
 We predict events in that new region,

Their replies foreshadowings
  Increasing   our self-regard.

  Of   their own convergences to come.
Think: this   future we have posited

Each celebration is more grand than the last.
   Is   the inescapable   site   of our death,

The   final   celebration,
The cause of our daily gloom.

Because of the slowing of movement,
   Narcissism   and hovering sadness –

Lies farther in the future
Hardly a way to live now.

Than the beginning   does in the distant past.
  So look to the past – not the past of causes,

At the present time,
But   origin-time.

Motions   on   every scale are modest,
 Look to birth and admiration, not

  Reflection is common,
To death and prediction.

And celebration   anticipated.
The end cannot but be kairotic birth.

History

Nothing   is more important
Branching ties us   together.

Than knowing how   far   back to go.
The   ancient songs, poems, and stories,

If you   do   not know this,
Rise up each buttressed trunk

You will not   know whom to blame,
From the earth. High   and   outward

And   if   you do   not   know *this*,
They move, across branch, twig, leaf –

You   will have no peace.
Through the   canopy.

Sumer: Literature and Women

We went   out of Erech with   Gilgamesh the   King,
They must   leave us alone. It's   horrible   that   he

We went to the Keeper of the Forest
Can do with us as he wishes. No one

To kill him, to cut his cedars down.
Can protect us, not our brothers, not

Brave Enkidu, lover of the King,
Our fathers or husbands. Even worse,

Turned back when we had done,
These men, our own kin, go

To pull out the roots; the roots
With the King. Well, good riddance

We had forgot to take.
To them. Forget them all.

We were strong and young.
They are not human.

. . . .

They shone, Gilgamesh and Enkidu;
  Women will prevail against power.

And Ishtar ruined them still.
Tenderness will prevail.

The goddess caused the lover a slow death.
Girls will be everywhere protected.

The King she denied eternal life
Our boys will become complete beings,

Through the immortal man,
   Not the incomplete fools

The Old Man behind the twin-breasted mountain.
Who scramble after those two, intent on death.

. . . .

We went out of Erech so long ago,
It will be a very long time coming,

Her great walls unblemished.
And men will be with us.

India: Justice and the Soul

The question is one of time.
I'm impatient, grandfather.

You in the West want
  I want to study.

What you call justice now, my dear.
  I want time for myself, to think.

You have not achieved justice
  I have talents, grandfather.

And you never will achieve it.
Have I not the right to have them?

You criticize us for our categorizations
  I understand how it is that our continuing

Of   all men and women. Unjust, you claim,
Our forebears' professions guarantees   a

Because there is no movement among our groupings.
 A sure form of   stability   for us,   daily   calm,

For you, "no movement," for us, assured choices, continuity.
  Relief from questions, from anxiety,   from   all ambiguity.

Yet there is movement for us.
  I   do not dispute   all that.

But   not in a "now."
There has been a price.

Movement   of   the soul from
   I   have thought about   it.

Body to   body   is the very process of achieving justice.
Can it be that the migration of a soul   from its past body

Each soul will ascend   as a   product   of its
  To   the next   is a man-made doctrine, devised

Last embodied acts, or   descend   similarly
   By   puritanical,   once quite violent men,

As a product of its   last embodied acts:
Later urbanized, who opposed any change,

 Justice over time,   the only   true justice.
"Justice over time" protecting their power?

 . . . .

Polysemy

If you insist on speaking of the now
I feel strange continuing in this way,

Rather than properly, over time,
But did these same men invent the soul?

Think of the range of our mental lives, right now:
 I don't know, I don't know, grandfather; I don't.

Several powerful logics, not one;
One of the reasons I'm confused is this:

An ancient and everyday-experienced creation of symbols,
What of mothers during the long domination of the fathers?

Where the West no longer knows what a symbol is.
Aren't mothers the cause of their children's happiness?

We have great richness of mind right now,
Would they have made what the fathers made,

And justice over time.
 Or not, dear grandfather?

China: The Cut Block and the Uncut Block

We have no choice but to make a cut
The first cut dividing the surface

On the clear surface of the block.
Of the block deeply wounds nature.

The first cut initiates correct thinking.
The beginning of the self-deception

It   permits the distinction
That plagues us endless talkers.

"This side of the cut,
  We begin to judge

That side of the cut."
  Representations

Before the cut we have only
To be the things they represent.

The bare, empty block, lacking thought.
Leave the block free of any   cut.

Wisdom consists   in wise cuts.
Life will take care of itself.

This is Wang Yang-ming:

"I love to remember what Meng Tzu said:

When any person, *any* person, sees a baby

Crawling toward a well, that person will be horrified

And will act instantly to save the baby.

I say, Yes,

When someone sees a baby crawling toward a well,

She becomes one with the baby.

Now a critic might say, That is so because

Both you and the baby are human beings.

I say, Yes, but

When someone sees a deer suffer,

She suffers, having become one with the deer.

The critic might say, Of course, because

Both you and the deer are warm-blooded animals.

I say, Yes, but

When someone sees a bird fall from its nest,

She suffers, having become one with the bird.

That critic won't stop: Naturally, because

Both you and the bird are living creatures.

I see, I see, but

What is to be made of this?

When someone sees rocks being crushed,

She feels crushed, having become one with rocks.

The critic falls silent.

Does this not mean

That all the entities in the universe,

Including us,

Are one and same substance?

That any of us can therefore

Become one with any entity?

Does that, in turn, not mean

That what the infinite universe is

And what human kindness is

Are One?"

Athens: Philosophy and Men

I am cursed by reason:
I work in   Laurion

 I   know I   will die.
With   thousands like me.

The   brutes in the field,
It's   dark in the mines.

Animal   and   human,
We go down and come out

Possess no   reason and bear no curse.
In the dark. I don't know what happened.

The   ages   before   my birth did not know me,
We're down there, that's all, and we'll either die   there

Polysemy

Nor will the ages after my death know me,
Or in the huts the citizens see fit

Unless, that is, my fame persists.
To provide for our families.

But what of the curse now?
What does meat taste like, huh?

. . . .

Reason produces and reason lifts the curse –
Our son worked in the mines with us; then he hurt

Of course!
His back.

All that I see and touch perishes,
Bad luck. My father hauls silver ore;

As I might have perished
That means that he can see

Had reason not fulfilled its promise.
The sun most days. Did you say that meat

For I have reasoned the imperishable,
Can give a person a bad stomach ache?

And more, I have become what I have reasoned.
I would like to try some anyway, I think.

Polysemy

The First Europe: Religion and Children

What you must remember, my son,
   I remember   my grandmother

Is that strict obedience, which is both a means
Letting us do whatever we liked all day long.

And an end, must be   inculcated
They were all   like that in our village.

From the very   beginning.
  All our babies are carried,

Obedience   is noble   and it is found everywhere,
When possible skin to skin, bouncing on our mothers' hips.

For the order   of things, the very placement   of   all
The older kids take care   of the younger ones when they

Entities   and processes, is   hierarchical,   as the B'rae Shees   teaches.
Start to run all over the place: what chaos, what fun. Our clan teaches these ways.

God the Father   is at the pinnacle,   of perfect substance.
Our fathers are much too demanding; "be   obedient,"

All   beneath are   of imperfect substance:
They say, and they punish us when we're not.

There, man reigns over   woman and child,
  Our   mothers aren't cruel; we cleave to them

Humanity   over   the animals,
And run away from our cruel fathers.

The animals above…you   understand me, my son, do you not?
The animals save us, but sometimes fathers do not understand.

Thus the child is taught to obey the father
Our puppies love us   unconditionally,

As humanity   is taught to obey   God the Father.
And they alert us to danger when they become grown up.

And to   what end? Our salvation.
Even though we ask nothing of them.

Still,   alas, our weakness demands
When our fathers are not   looking

Threat as well as reward.
We "become" our totems.

Proclaim eternal   bliss after   earthly   sorrow
Giving us double substance in the here and now.

Wherever   you travel,
And closeness to others

And proclaim   eternal pain for the   disobedient.
Who become the same totem animals – our clanspeople.

How blessed is   early   death;
How good our lives can be.

The sooner does bliss begin,
We love to live a long time,

Never to end.
To enjoy life.

This for all   humanity
But fathers call our totems

 For God   is One.
"Gods," with contempt.

Resist false gods, and   particularly
So yet   again   we run from our fathers,

Those who worship many gods,
  So we can live   the old way.

For these are the worst of men,
We want to live happily

Doomed forever   to hellfire.
And we know how to do that.

The Second Europe: Science and Children

Natural   languages are imprecise.
Please tell me   a story,   grandmother.

They may be   suitable   for stories,
I'm scared to   go to sleep without one.

But   for nothing serious.
Would you include a giraffe?

Polysemy

The calculus now permits us unparalleled precision,
  I got confused in school again. They laughed at me. Am I dumb?

Unlimited present application,
At recess today we played dodge-ball.

Unknowable future development.
Athletic boys always aim to hit me.

Such power!
Am I bad?

To locate an element horizontally
The homework on Wednesday gave me a headache.

On one abcissa,
Memorizing things,

Vertically on another;
Really hard arithmetic,

To compute the attraction of two masses
Writing about places that don't mean anything.

As the product of a constant,
Why can't I play the way I want?

The two masses in question,
Be a seagull, grandmother,

And the inverse of their distance squared –
And I'll be a great big humpbacked whale!

Such   elegance!
That'll be funny!

. . . .

Universal truths.
Isn't it okay

Immortal particles.
Just that I am alive?

Contemporaneity: Commerce and the Human Condition

Thank goodness for the graceful ships out of Venice
I've always loved the water. So has my sister.

So many centuries ago.
As children we would splash and play

They brought goods back to Europe
And laugh in the rain, in ponds,

From such distances as would
In the nearby lake, being

Mystify Europeans about their worth.
As silly as baby ducks, with no burdens,

So the tradesmen of those mysterious goods
No thought of the past or worrisome future.

Polysemy

Could price them as they wished,
    Water   was   innocence.

First   extolling   them,   inventing   a   past
Why are humpback whales beaching themselves now?

That buyers could   not possibly check   on.
 Why   do adults   interfere with   the   whales?

. . . .

The ancient skill   of   divining   another's thoughts,
Our grandmothers can know what we   are   feeling   as

Conscious and unconscious thoughts,
  We feel   it,   immediately.

From time   immemorial   employed in the   other's interests
They know; and only then do they decide how to help   us best.

Was   now employed to   fix   the highest price
They would   never   use their gift   selfishly.

A   buyer was   willing   to pay.
But grandmothers are asked   go to

Nothing was   so   perfectly   calculated
Nursing homes! What arguments can justify

Since   the very invention of   coinage
This, their   separation from children?

In   the Aegean   basin –
How solemn we've become,

The concretization of calculation itself.
How divorced from childhood play and the dignity of age.

. . . .

In time we would price every object on every scale
We want reciprocity back: all gifts, the very same value,

And every process in time,
All of us, the same value,

Still mystifying, ever extolling,
Since each of us is a gift to others.

Celebrating calculative virtuosity.
Commerce is like science, isn't it? Overdevelopment,

When calculation is not directed to profit,
Overvaluation, disequilibrium,

It is given to victory in contests.
Insult to what lies deepest in consciousness,

Is not a successful sale too a victory?
  Elevating triviality, a threat to life.

Polysemy

A Dialogue^{Dialogue}

A garret in Paris, 1822. John Keats escaped death in 1821.

JOHN

The weight of twice your years
My limbs   remain   heavy,

Burdens me, Tom.
My breath is slow.

As strength returns, my game with death –
Will I   regain   my former   strength?

Such pain conjoined for   most of   us with age, not youth –
I'm young   and I   know far   too   much of   suffering.

Is cause to feel   excess of age.
I wish to know no more of it.

Tom Keats died in 1818.

TOM

Dear   brother,
You're weary;

When I   tell you   what you surely know,
I   pray   that you'll soon be what you were.

That you're absurdly   far from twice my age,
When we   were children, no one outstripped you.

My aim is not to count your years
You were always our   good   knight,

But to ignore   such arid   numbers –
Our champion among the dangers

As you yourself   ignore them in your claim –
Of our childhood, our Arthur   Pendragon.

And   tell   you that you're half my age,
Were you ten,   perhaps,   becoming

And half of that – a child,
Every   object   you saw?

Undiminished   by   passing   time.
And then laughing? Your laughter buoyed

Full in mind among these crowds of emptied men.
Us up, filling us   with your   joy in living.

JOHN

So only you would say, Tom.
Enough of   my   self-pity.

TOM

I, or you, would say…ah, bother.
Which is it? I   think… Oh well,

It's   often   that we   cannot voice our secret thoughts.
Thoughts or words, presence or absence, you or we,   both.

But words have now been said,
Your (or   our) gratitude

Even   if in silence…
Cannot be exceeded.

JOHN

...as "upon a peak in Darien?"
Was it last of night or first of day?
A sleepless watcher of the skies...

TOM

As upon a peak in Darien.
It retains its hold on our heart.

JOHN

But what is brought to life
I am a beginner;

By opening the book of mind
I know so little of life

To put beside great Homer's lines?
Beyond my meager experience.

TOM

More than Attic verse and meter,
How odd that you misunderstand,

More than Attic hero's brutal force:
Who understands more than anyone.

The very shape of mind itself,
You enlarge, not simply reveal

At birth complete,
Our endowment,

Its fate to sing.
Its very song.

Joseph Severn enters; he has remained with Keats.

JOSEPH

Hesitant　　to leave
You remain fragile;

Even for　a　moment,
Anything can happen.

I　　feared relapse.
Wait…improvement.

But here you are, your brow returned
A　　greater　　wakefulness,　I think;

To thought, from pain.
The John　　of　old.

JOHN

Which I owe to you, dear friend.
A　　debt I　cannot　　repay.

JOSEPH

Not to　　　me;　to fortune
We could have been too late.

And to　the　　span and depth
But you live, John, you live!

 Of　a　spirit　　wounded
Consumption did not win.

But　　indominable.
Your spirit triumphed.

JOHN

Joseph,   Joseph…
How good you are.

Kindness heals.
Your   presence

Your kindly ministrations
And   your kindly attentions

Healed all the wounds of which you speak
To   the   embarrassments   of   mind

And became a   part of my course of life.
No   less than of   a   body   in   ruins.

JOSEPH

To become a part of your…
How can I respond to such…

John, I think I know
Let   me take a breath.

How   and when your genius
Now. This   is   my   theory:

Grew to   such a size
   I poured over each

As the world will soon
Poem   following

Announce to constitute
The   draft of Hyperion.

The   most complete   poetic gift
A   profound change had taken place,

Mankind has known.
A   miracle.

It was Tom…
The secret…

JOHN

How I   miss him, Joseph.
I'll   not   release   you, Tom.

JOSEPH

Your grief upon his death,
  Unimaginable   pain;

Your imperious grief…
  I   too was undone.

But in   the heat of many weeks
During that time with your brother,

Ever   by his   bedside, feeling
Thinking nothing of your own health,

Every gasp of breath and wrenching cough,
Entirely   understanding   the danger,

You wrote   *Hyperion.*
You fused your two souls.

As you   suffered, you wrote.
Sustained by your   writing –

As Tom was dying,
Writing   as   never

You brought his spirit
  Before,   his spirit

Into   your own,   becoming twice
Augmenting yours, your own transformed

What you had been.
    Into   poetry –

Hyperion   became your work and his,
One now two, freed from the dross of days,

As the Odes would be,
Free indeed   to   loft

A monument built
Above us all, free,

By both   of you as one.
Doubled, and immortal.

JOHN

If what you say is true
I felt what you describe.

Then Tom and I will gladly
The   former 'I' now 'we,'

Share such authorship
Alchemically   bound

As the future brings.
In a   new alloy.

JOSEPH

I'm put in mind
The Symposium…

Of Socrates –
Unequalled

No poet but…
In its time…

JOHN

…though philosophizing
You range widely, Joseph.

Poetizes in its way.
A poetry of thought.

JOSEPH

The philosophy to which I refer
Plato is the supreme philosopher.

Is that of silence.
Only he understood

Socratic silence
The nature of thought;

Calls up for me *To Autumn*,
So you understand poetry,

Both by doubled minds.
As arising from –

For Socrates would stand in trance,
What shall I say – doubled silence.

Attending two internal voices,
Standing in the bustling agora,

Simultaneous voices,
Deaf to importunate voices,

That spoke his deepest thoughts to him alone.
Plato has Socrates talk to himself,

How could he not distrust
But   not   as   you or I

Both speech and writing,
Would talk   to ourselves.

For how could thought, *doubled,*
His two,   different   voices

Suit   the speech or writing
Would speak   at   the same time –

That   merely moves a *single* word,
And he heard them   as a third voice,

One after the last?
Larger and silent.

JOHN

I never knew
 Admirable!

How deeply   read
We   have both read

In Plato's work you are.
The Greeks to advantage,

I   see your doubled Socrates.
You to philosophical depth.

JOSEPH

I'm compelled to wonder, John,
Plato   also   ponders on

Whether   singularity,
Whether what we take as "one"

The state that   all   but you must suffer,
Is   in   truth "half,"   whatever   our eyes

Is   deprivation.
Tell us is the case.

JOHN

Singularity   deprivation?
We must not trust our senses in this matter.

It's   surely so.
They deceive us.

You said   "empty men."
A   man may seem whole

They are merely one
To   us   and others,

When to be complete
But   be   incomplete.

Must be to be two in one.
The   aspiration   is clear –

But emptiness is not their choice;
An aspiration   often   blocked

The superficial lives that other men,
By the mean-spiritedness of others.

With meager hearts,
They   are   victims,

Have thrust upon them,
Unable   to   see

Have drained them dry.
Their   oppression.

A heart must seek and   occupy another heart
The   recovery   of one's fullest personhood

That a doubled life might grow.
Restores true vision, and strength.

JOSEPH

We must not   despise them, then,
But how much fault lies with them?

But   pity them.
Some? but little?

JOHN

Better help   than pity,
Don't worry about fault;

Don't you think, Joseph?
Everyone   needs help.

JOSEPH

Yes, to help,
Help we must,

Each as he can.
Fault or no fault.

You, John, in   *Hyperion*
No   one   has been of such help

And the Odes,
As   you have.

Take each   one of us
"Doubling" is a word,

On roads of plangent words and pauses
But your   poetry   acts, changing us,

To our second selves,
Helping us to   see

There to see   as   if in undisturbed   water,
The   greater selves until that time hidden from sight,

Ourselves enlarged.
Pulsing   with life.

JOHN

Perhaps the poet shares
I   believe   Plato

With medicine,   my first vocation,
Is   more healer than philosopher.

The ancient Hippocratic urge:
Perhaps the   poet also   heals.

To heal.
Perhaps.

JOSEPH

I assure   you, John,
There can be no   doubt.

That while you suffered from consumption,
You don't know that I   was your patient,

And then in time defeated it,
That during your suffering,

Your body coming back to you,
You oversaw my suffering,

My own spirit,
And ended it.

Shrunk at first and wounded,
Whispered fragments healed me.

Was healed by verses that you spoke
So we recovered together,

With at first depleted breath.
My strength drawn from your verse.

JOHN

Reciprocity, dear friend?
I owe you more than you owe me.

JOSEPH

No restoration of health
I could not remain with you

In one direction
Without descending

Maintains its way
With you, in mind

Unless there comes to be
As well as in body.

A movement in return.
Without conscious willing,

Restoration, like the mind,
You nursed me while I nursed you.

Is too a doubling.
   Reciprocity.

JOHN

We see a child, but we do not,
How noble of you to insist.

For there *is* no "child"
I see that doublings

But "the mother and child combined."
Abound; you are wise to insist.

JOSEPH

I believe there is no "person"
Your example is apposite.

But "the person and much loved friend combined."
Permit me to add friendship to kinship?

JOHN

Yes, "and much loved friend."
You're right to say so.

JOSEPH

I'll see who it is.
Who is knocking?

TOM

Never would I have guessed
If you have added me,

That Joseph thinks so well.
Joseph has added you.

JOHN

His cheer and whimsy
His   earlier   self

Fooled us.
Has grown.

TOM

Taking   you to Rome
He proved   resourceful

Began his growth.
In   Italy.

JOHN

And   *understanding* Rome.
Much more than resourceful.

Empire, arms, and law;
Rome's accomplishments

Surfaces   and the light
Are admired over much.
Can such light blind us?

We thought were all in all.
Size   and   force are nothing.

But   here, in France,
Paris, though younger,

To   which he'd gone before,
Proves to   suit us   better.

And, again, understood:
Great age does not mean depth.

Not millennia of time
Rome mastered controlling men

And the classical pulse of Rome,
And domesticated Greek art –

Shallow in its feeling.
Hardly admirable.

Rather here, in Paris
The precedent for depth

Nine or ten centuries ago,
In Paris goes back to Abelard

The medieval heart of France
And to Bernard of Clairvaux,

Expressed the roots of feeling.
To their opposed views of life.

Not arms, argument, and light,
The true span of Rome was small,

But mystery, art, and shadow.
The span of Paris, majestic.

TOM

Poetry seeks the dark.
Truth lies in shadows.

When we cannot see,
What we see deceives.

We imagine greatly.
The   imagination

Light reveals the fixed and literal,
 Precedes arrogant   calculation.

What the dark reveals is ever-changing,
Shadows   encourage   transformation

Forms becoming other forms
And   accumulation.

As our minds in   churning fullness wish.
Thus are our minds granted their freedom.

Marcel Rogin is a sixty-year-old Parisian flaneur.

JOSEPH

It   was   Marcel   at the door.
Good cheer has come to see   us.

JOHN

 I'm glad to see you, Marcel.
Now for the news of   Paris.

MARCEL

And   I   you, my dear Keats.
Phew, I'm quite out of breath.

I've come with much to tell you.
But   excitement,   excitement!

JOHN

Good. Please sit. Do.
 Do   calm yourself.

MARCEL

I've been to such a house
Five, ten minutes ago…

Of miracles, my friends,
I couldn't believe it.

As I never could imagine.
Who could have thought of such a thing?

What I have seen
But I saw it!

Will lift your hearts.
How marvelous!

JOHN

You make me curious beyond bearing.
What wonderful enthusiasm.

MARCEL

You, John, will see it all.
You will see what I saw.

A house in the Rue St. Jacques,
Wait…tell the story calmly:

A school, where the deaf
First, the school itself.

Are taught to make their inner lives
Now, can the deaf communicate?

Clear to others without speech.
That's the question – without speech!

A   miraculous   place,
You will not believe this.

For silence –
Not a sound,

But hands and face in rapid,
But movements of stirring speed

Wondrous gesture –
Carrying meanings.

Proves to   say more than words,
Yet   more! The gestures   seem

I   think, can say.
To reach beyond

More than words, gentlemen.
What mere words can suggest.

JOSEPH

You speak to the master of the word, Rogin.
What gall   to assert such nonsense to John Keats.

JOHN

Wait, dear Joseph, wait.
Not   nonsense, Joseph.

Marcel   comes in good   spirit,
This news, yes, Marcel's surmise,

His news a   marvel.
May portend something

How more than words, Marcel?
Of   great   significance.

MARCEL

Let me take a   step
History…..that's it.

Back to Bonaparte's Egyptian venture.
Bonaparte   was interested   in things,

The signs he found,
Dusty   objects,

The silent hieroglyphic signs,
Old hieroglyphic inscriptions.

In principle   divorced from sound,
Hieroglyphs could not be spoken –

Each, I now am   certain, contains
Just   as a   deaf man can not speak –

A   cornucopia,   gentlemen:
But each sign points to many things,

Meanings pouring forth
To   many   objects

As long as one might contemplate the sign.
Or events   or whole, lengthy narratives.

The mind fills…
   Ecstasy!

JOHN

By the gods…
Can this be?

MARCEL

What it is I come to say is this:
Long-ago Egypt and Paris now:

The gestures made by hands and face
Two   silences   eons   apart,

In   the Rue St. Jacques,
Both true   plenitudes!

Like the emblems
We learn to read

Carved in high relief
The   inscriptions;

Beside   the Sphinx,
We learn to   read

Offer   *their*   plenitudes   in silence.
The signs made by the hands of the deaf.

JOHN

How came such a thing to be?
This must be thought of with care.

MARCEL

Aware of your boundless sympathy,
    If anyone   can understand this,

Nothing could please me more than to   tell   you
    It certainly   will be   you, my dear Keats.

Whence the miracle   comes.
  And surprised you will be!

It's not from   dry instruction,
From schooling? That is absurd.

Not from quiet rumination,
Introspection?   Not at all.

Nor from Christian inspiration; but
  Religion?   I laugh heartily. Now!

From the poor and wild young of Paris,
Who would suspect the truth of all this?

Who, deaf, despised, long   ago   created
Deaf children, Keats; deaf children created

Their own   effective   speech,
Their own language, their own,

The speech of hands.
 Made of   gestures.

The Rue St. Jacques has made
I   derided   schooling,

Of this   a matter to be taught
Meaning traditional schooling.

To those who do not know it,
But in   compassionate schools?

And indeed, I think, to such as hear
Everyone,   I think, if   instructed

But think the hands can   complement   the voice;
To   communicate   with both hands and voice

For   everyone,   perhaps, would flourish
Would be happier! Saying   more, hearing

Knowing what only Egypt knew...
Everything, like the Egyptians.

JOHN

Egypt and the city's poor…
How unlikely a pairing.

Neither wealth nor genius
Whom are we to respect?

Has granted such a gift to humankind
In children lie all the gifts of the mind

As these children have –
Crying out to live.

By bravely claiming their right
These children have each other

To live as human beings.
Completely, mind to mind.

JOSEPH

It's a wonder, John, certainly.
Too much excitement, all this talk.

But the time has come
You're not recovered.

For you to rest.
Slow your thinking.

Marcel and I will leave you now.
You've been stimulated enough.

Quiet your mind
I'll be back.

And   rest.
Please rest.

MARCEL

Good day, then, Keats.
I'll   take   my   leave.

This has   been enough – a
My words have tumbled out;

Taxing   visit,   perhaps,
I was possessed, I think.

Requiring   assimilation.
We'll return to this discovery.

JOHN

Good bye   to you   both.
I   must think this through.

TOM

A new day.
Astounding.

JOHN
I sense a new beginning.
A source of new energies.
Do I   awake to the dark?

I   have wondered,
What is my place?

What can I be to Shakespeare?
The   apex belongs to   him.

What he   to me?
How would he have

I   believe I soon will know.
Judged   my poetry 'til   now?

Joseph…
Welcome.

JOSEPH

I'm sorry, John.
I'm back too soon.

I'd planned to leave the letter.
I'm   forgetful,   I'm afraid.

JOHN

I'm always glad to see you, Joseph.
You need never apologize   to me.

Besides, I sleep too much.
I'd rather be   awake.

A   letter, you say?
From whom, I wonder.

JOSEPH

From Fanny Brawne.
I   fear distress.

JOHN

Let me see   it.
I see it's brief.

She says she still   does not
I'm   sorry   she   complains

Understand why it   is we stay.
Of our   remaining in Paris.

JOSEPH

May I say more of her
I cannot   remain mute.

Than has been my habit?
I   felt   that my respect

I never wished –
For your person

I never   will wish –
And for your poetry

To trouble you with idle   talk.
Called for reticence about her.

But I've thought these months
I've   reread   your poems

At home, on sea, and
In the   setting of

In Rome and here,
All   our   poetry

Of your place in history.
As far   as   I know of it,

I   cannot bear   to see that   place
And what compares with what you've done?

Put under threat   by the   importunities
Nothing, no one, must now interfere with you.

Of lesser persons,
Do not permit it.

Even when what may appear
Your finer　nature　must not

A criticism　of your part
Play　so　ironic　a　part,

Must be brought to　light.
　　Impeding　　your work.

JOHN

Trusting your circumspection, then,
I could　not　have more confidence

Tell me, Joseph –
In　your judgment.

Fanny…
Tell me…

JOSEPH

You were over-mastered
This　is　how I　assess

By　　impulse.
Most young men

Miss Brawne is and will　remain
And　　certainly　young women:

Moved to　and　　fro herself by impulse.
Although grown and seemingly mature,

But what for you was passing,
But only physically so,

In her will never change.
Young persons everywhere,

For that brief time, only then,
Still essentially children,

You were in fact alike.
Show little true judgment

You are now another person.
And no rein over their desires.

She will never see you
Miss Brawne did not know you

As you've become,
As you are now.

And unseen, you will chafe.
Now in full maturity,

But loyal and determined to squelch
Your kindness and large-spiritedness

Your yearning to be seen,
Might fasten you to her

You will stay with her.
    Indefinitely.

Never let that happen.
Never let that happen!

Never, I beg.
I beg you, John.

JOHN

But…do   I not love her?
I   hear, but I'm confused.

JOSEPH

Impulse of youth
   Definitions…

Is   always called
A   false meaning;

And   wrongly called love.
The word should be dropped.

JOHN

Advise   me, Joseph.
What then shall I do?

JOSEPH

Let   some months go by,
Wait. Let   healing time

Here, in Paris.
Pass   slowly.

You will   grow,
You have grown,

She will not.
She has not.

Each   will understand the other in time,
There need be no anger between you two.

And you will go your different ways.
Your lives should in no way be conjoined.

The reasons to converge
The past predicts nothing,

Are passed.
 Nothing.

The reasons to diverge instead,
To be free to live as you must

Will multiply.
 Is everything.

JOHN

Paris has become a refuge for us,
I have loved my life in these apartments.

These twisting streets and ancient stones.
The little I have roamed about

The shadows of which you've spoken
Has already redirected

Are dark harbors where
My meditations

Ghostly ships arrive and stay,
On words, things, and poetry,

Awaiting me to plumb their holds.
To ends I cannot now foresee.

How it may become
Perhaps it will be

For her and me?
Better for her,

We'll wait, and see.
   Better   for me...

A table outside a small restaurant on the Rue St. Jacques.

MARCEL

To think that Keats was near
A   tragedy   for art,

His death at twenty-five.
The worst of tragedies!

JOSEPH

He'd found his stride
So   short   a   time

A year   before his   health gave way.
To have accomplished such wonders.

From one autumn to the next
The   annus mirabilis

He wrote the greatest lyrics yet composed .
In   the   history   of English poetry.

MARCEL

When you kindly   brought the Odes to   me
  To say the truth,   I   enjoy few poems.

I   felt   at once the rarest joy,
But these! Immediate rapture!

An elevation   to spheres
Thinking is not my strong suit,

That know no measured time or   space.
But feelings like these lift my thoughts

To   lift   a   fellow man to such a place…
With them to heights I had never attained.

JOSEPH

…to lift the world itself.
  He is   universal.

MARCEL

Is he happy, Severn?
I wish him happiness.

JOSEPH

He lives when he sits to write.
Writing   is   his   happiness.

At other times he sucks up more
  But he uses   other times well,

Of what he finds around him
 Becoming   whatever   he

Than anyone can fathom.
Turns his   attention to.

MARCEL

A "more" that   comprehends
What surrounds one includes

Both what can serve
   Nutrients,   true,

And what can wreck him?
But poisons   as   well.

JOSEPH

You've sensed the problem rightly.
Quite perceptive, I must say.

Keats is loath to push away
He is overgenerous –

Even what will   weaken him.
Which challenges his judgment.

MARCEL

It's difficult when young
That is   forgivable.

To   know   what *gives* to one
Youth means   daily   mistakes.

And the opposite, what *steals* from one.
All   of that can be   repaired, with luck.

His judgment will mature.
Ah, I   have   my methods…

JOSEPH

Of course it will.
All   will   be well.

Until that time, his happiness
There is   no mystery in this;

Will lie with poetry   alone.
John will write without hindrance.

MARCEL

I   can but infer
There's a woman here.

From hints that you and he
  I   cannot be deceived

Have inadvertently   let slip
About affairs of the young heart;

That a woman comes between
  A woman is   causing pain

Dear Keats and happiness.
 For   our convalescent.

JOSEPH

As   frequently is the case,
How true; a woman indeed.

The remedy *appears* to be
The cliché is, "reunite them,"

The joining of the two
  A   terrible   idea.

Whom circumstances
   On the contrary,

Have cruelly separated.
They must be separated

It is poverty
Permanently.

Of judgment to think
The real question is

That such conjoining
How to   achieve that

Will bring about their happiness.
   Without my badly hurting John.

No, to wait is best.
I pray he   listens.

MARCEL

Well, young man,
Hah,   the   time

There's more than that to   say.
   Is   ripe   for me to spring!

To wait: perhaps.
Joseph,   my boy,

But what of empty waiting?
Have you no imagination?

JOSEPH

Not   so for Keats.
What do you mean?

He'll write.
He'll write.

MARCEL

Yes, he'll write.
Yes, yes,   yes;

But   don't you want
That's not the point.

Ecstasies   of other kinds for John Keats?
There's more to life, my puritanical   friend.

JOSEPH

Of course I do.
You need not ask.

MARCEL

Perhaps the woman whom
Need I say that women

You see a danger to him
Differ dramatically?

Can be displaced.
There are women

Great spirits come to us
And there are real *women.*

In skirts as well as britches, Severn.
Hah, I know much more about such things

Our Voltaire knew this perfectly,
Than these boys could possibly know,

And flourished best
So I suppose

When in company with a woman
I must forgive this naïf Severn.

His equal in perspicacity.
I suspect he will presently learn.

JOSEPH

We   in Britain
What? Another

Little   think of women thus.
Woman flailing in our midst?

Assertion stays with men.
The role of woman   is

Great achievement comes from us.
To   give support   and   comfort

Is that   not so in   France?
To man: so it must   stay.

MARCEL

Largely yes, it's so.
Alas,   true enough.

Exceptions, however,
     Generalizations

Are scarcely few.
Can conceal truths.

Away   from academic study,
Men's clubs remain closed to novelty.

Which remains a male preserve,
Perhaps power makes us stale.

The   salon, the space of women,
Women, with less power, can think.

Scintillates with thought.
There is no   salon

I myself would never lapse attendance,
That does not surprise me wonderfully –

So stimulating are salon nights.
Not to mention ogling the women.

JOSEPH

I'm astonished, Rogin.
Do I hear correctly?

MARCEL

A splendid woman,
At last I can speak.

Vivienne Bonnot,
A fine woman.

Versed in English,
Accomplished in

And German, too,
Literature,

Has more than sung
Sensitive to

Sweet praise of Keats;
Supreme poetry,

She has understood him.
Overawed by John's Odes.

Her soul and his
They are like twins,

Are tuned alike.
Each unknown to

Each can dwell
The　　other,

In another's thoughts,
Waiting to   entwine

And look upon
Their inner lives

The other's　 vista.
In newfound gladness.

JOSEPH

Marcel, have you prepared an argument?
You have　 obviously　　waited for this.

Does this Vivienne Bonnot
Well, who　 is this　 woman?

Aspire　　to   meet our friend?
What does she want with Keats?

MARCEL

Mademoiselle Bonnot –
Calm yourself, Joseph.

Good Vivienne –
The　 fact is

Only　 she can match our friend,
We may have a　　paradox

Not in　　 composition
Welcome to your judgment.

But in kindness.
She will never

So she will not presume.
  Interfere with our John.

JOSEPH

It's you,   I   see, who wishes
She has sense; you   do   not.

Keats and her to meet.
Why   do you trouble?

MARCEL

I   think perhaps our matchless John
Our very great   but weakened friend

Has had surfeit   of   girls.
Will get nothing from girls,

As large a mind as   Keats commands,
But that does not mean that   he needs

Recognition   by a   woman, not a girl,
Nothing that a woman is prepared to give.

Giving back to   him
You do not know that;

A woman's tenderness,
I doubt that he knows it.

Will warm that mind
    Experience

And keep him glad
Has taught me this:

To   meet each day.
Men need women.

JOSEPH

Can   any other,
Keats is complete;

Man or   woman,
He needs no one.

Bring to Keats
He   must be

A view of things
Left to   himself

Unknown to him?
To   live   his life.

MARCEL

One sets one's vision   forward
Do   we   have two, three, four heads?

Or to   the   side –
 Silly young man.

Never everywhere   at once, Severn.
Your William Blake's fourfold   vision –

It can't   be done.
You see? I   have

A   woman looks
Good taste in books –

Where   men do   not,
 Comes when men and

And looks with woman's eyes.
 Women   look   together.

JOSEPH

You say that Keats
Can I be wrong?

Allied with someone,
Can John be happier?

A woman…
Someone else…

MARCEL

…whose judgment is commodious…
… by no means not just anyone…

JOSEPH

…might gain
…might add

The full circumference
Something valuable?

To which you refer.
Indispensable?

MARCEL

I do.
Of course!

JOSEPH

I will contemplate
I won't close my mind

The possibility.
Against his happiness.

It's up to him, however.
If someone can help him,

It's Keats who will choose
As Marcel suggests,

To know whomever he wants to know.
I would certainly not interfere.

MARCEL

If Keats is asked
An opening?

By me, perhaps, to see her,
I will ask Keats to see her.

He'll not refuse:
He must agree;

His kindness will not permit it.
He is too kind not to agree.

But she would not presume:
Vivienne, on the other

Her kindness will not permit it.
Hand, for the same reason, will not

So rest at ease, my boy.
Agree to see our Keats.

They'll never meet.
So? A stalemate.

Marcel sits opposite Vivienne Bonnot at the same table on the following day.

VIVIENNE

Oh my, Marcel, I hope
Have you been rash, Marcel?

You didn't approach him
What impression would

On my account.
You give of me?

I would die before
You know how I feel.

Delaying his recovery.
I would never distress John Keats.

MARCEL

No no, Vivienne.
Don't worry, dear.

It was Severn I approached –
Severn was trouble enough,

A most protective friend to Keats,
A walking barrier to others,

In fact, a barrier
Including allies.

Of some dimension.
Annoying fellow.

VIVIENNE

I'm glad he has a friend
Keats deserves such a friend

So obstinate.
Protecting him.

In Severn's place,
I would do so.

I'd find it in myself
No one would trouble him

To be a martinet.
Were I his protector.

MARCEL

Indeed: you would have built
You frighten me with your…

A wall no interloper dared to climb.
　Your ferocity, you gentle enemy

Would you have barred yourself?
　Of your friends' enemies.

VIVIENNE

A paradox, Marcel.
I am that wall's builder,

As his friend, I'd *have*
You silly Marcel.

His company.
He would need me

It's others I would keep from him.
To maintain the barrier's service.

MARCEL

Vivienne,   I must adopt
 Enough. To the question:

A more severe position.
You are the exact person

It's only   good that you
Keats needs to complete him,

Would bring to him; I know this,
   As   Keats is the   one person

Though you do not.
    Who can truly

Defer   to me, dear woman.
Bring you the joy you deserve.

VIVIENNE

Let us talk of something else, Marcel.
  I am torn between two life courses.

MARCEL

I   apologize,   Mademoiselle.
I must take care not   to go too far.

I'd be   very   sorry
Vivienne's friendship means too

To   offend.
Much to me.

VIVIENNE

You've not offended me.
   No   my dear Marcel;

I must simply think awhile
You always intend the best

About our meeting, Keats and I.
For your friends – with such charming guile.

But you and I have more to think about.
Now: there is something much more important

You brought Sicard to his attention?
To do. You spoke of sign language?

MARCEL

I did, to both of them.
I was quite triumphant.

I spoke with heartfelt admiration
My eloquence? an inspiration.

Of brilliant work his school has done
The nobility of his work

With many struck with silence.
Demanded sublime language .

VIVIENNE

And of his limits, as you put it?
For you his work goes only so far.

MARCEL

It's you who thinks
I'm a skeptic.

Sicard's conviction that the deaf
Sicard understands the limits

Can only walk a certain distance
Of his methods as perhaps you don't,

On the road they wish to travel –
My dear, and I defer to him.

That such a judgment is incorrect.
Do you not base your hopeful judgment

I agree with him.
On love of children?

VIVIENNE

A great achievement
True discoveries

Can include a great mistake, Marcel.
Are often mixed in implications.

His is that the deaf
His discovery

Can never reach the full
Could inhibit further

Humanity of those who hear.
Progress for those who cannot hear.

MARCEL

You believe they can.
You are quite certain.

VIVIENNE

I know it.
Certainly.

Remember Condillac.
Condillac suggested

He wrote of all this.
Not mere parity

A fully silent language
Of the hearing and the deaf,

Of hands and face, he wrote at last,
But the superiority

Could be, as I recall his phrase,
Of deaf communication :

"A language of simultaneous ideas."
Complete exchanges of all our deepest thoughts.

We can't comprehend such a thing as this.
What a wonderment such a thing would be!

If one among us all
An immense breadth of mind

Can grasp the consequence
Will be required to grasp

Of Condillac's assertion,
This potentiality

It will be Keats.
Concretely: Keats!

MARCEL

I touched upon it then:
    Simultaneity.

The force of hands,
Two routes to it,

Like the force of hieroglyphs,
Both   silent, for eyes alone.

Creating   plenitudes.
Pure amazement to me,

Keats was moved.
 And   to   Keats.

VIVIENNE

Of course he was.
Could it   have been

Still, to hear such things described
 Otherwise for   such   genius?

Can not compare with
But he must see them;

Intimate   experience   of them.
He must see the movement of hands,

He has not learned – not yet learned –
The stillness of   inscriptions.

The signs of hands and face;
What effects they   will have

Nor the signs of ancient Egypt.
We can scarcely   imagine.

MARCEL

I   wonder   if
Will Keats think so?

He'll take them up.
One   never knows.

VIVIENNE

He will.
He will!

Until   that time,
And now, Marcel,

There's something you must do.
　An　　important　　errand.

MARCEL

I'm   at your service, Vivienne.
Now I'm in　　my element.

VIVIENNE

Take Keats to Notre Dame
This   music will conjoin

When Perotin   is being sung.
Moving hands and still inscriptions.

MARCEL

The   great   motets!
Quelle joie, Vivienne!

Who else   but   you could
The   ear serves the eye:

Join Sicard to   Bonaparte –
　A   music of those mute signs,

The   signs of   flying hands to   those of Egypt's scribes –
Those changing as we look, those fixed in   time's amber,

In the nave of Notre Dame,
In a space of mutation,

Where different texts
Where more emerges

Are put to different tunes –
Than was first introduced.

All performed at once.
The perfect setting!

VIVIENNE

Everyone believes
So few think well…

That modern ears reject
We hear more than we think,

Such simultaneity.
And comprehend what we hear.

But Perotin, so long ago,
The old Magisters understood.

Assumed a wide reception
They needed a large music,

Both of words and tones,
Never heard before,

Enfolding every strand of thought and feeling.
For a space never before experienced.

And more than hearing all of this,
Their insight -- simultaneity

Hearing in between those lines,
And confidence in the mind's

The unheard thoughts,
Unused   powers.

The tones not sung.
Sound in   silence.

MARCEL

What splendid minds they had
  They were giants   back then,

When Notre Dame was built.
    Centuries   ago.

VIVIENNE

We   have them still,
There is   no   loss,

But half of mind now sleeps.
  Only   forgetfulness.

MARCEL

You're telling   me
  The whole mind wakes.

That Keats, awake,
  If   any   mind

Will hear   it   all.
Is   whole, it's his!

VIVIENNE

He   will.
Of course.

And   Perotin's motets,
From three new directions,

The silent gestures of the deaf,
New fruit, hitherto untended,

And Egypt's hieroglyphs,
Will gratefully flourish

Finding homes in him,
And   surprise us all

Will, like seeds,
With such life

Ripen into   masterworks
As the ages yearned to know

Of which   humanity
And will at last possess

Can only dream.
 And celebrate.

MARCEL

I will take him there,
I will waste no time.

And   tell him
He'll know all.

Whose advice I follow.
What gratitude he'll feel!

VIVIENNE

No, Marcel.
Say nothing.

We act   for him,
He must not think

In   no respect for   me.
That I would trouble him.

MARCEL

I act   for   both.
Nothing stops me!

The garret.

JOHN

This letter, Tom,
   Interesting…

How am I   to think about it?
Does it mean what   it announces:

How shall I regard its claims?
   A   new   sensibility

More than courtesy informs it, surely.
   Associated   with my poetry?

TOM

And more than elevated taste.
She   is   as much historian

To place your work so firmly in
As   vigorous   advocate,

 In   the flow of time.
Showing where you stand.

Listen   once again to what she writes:
You are understood by this   woman.

"This is not a moment, dear Mister Keats,

Merely in the history of your or our literatures,

Or indeed of literature as such.

This is a moment in the history of humanity.

Champollion is here, now,

Unconcealing the mind of ancient Egypt –

Not "another language,"

But another *kind* of language.

Sicard is here, now,

Unconcealing the minds of those

Who cannot hear –

Again, another *kind* of language.

Notre Dame is here,

Where counterpoint and words are joined together.

And my dear Mister Keats,

You are here, alone equipped

To gather all of this and make them one.

Remain with us, I beg you."

JOHN

Her   enthusiasm   takes one's breath away.
"To gather all of this   and   make   them one…"

TOM

Fanny   writes to importune you home.
One young woman thinks but of herself,

Her plan for married life
Of   mere appearances

Requires you home.
Back in   England.

Mademoiselle Bonnot writes
 The   other   young woman

To   importune   you stay.
Thinks of you, yes, but more,

Humanity,   she says, requires that
Of all of us, and she   has   a plan.

You join Champollion, Sicard, and Perotin,
She knows that you can absorb the genius

To synthesize and add to   them
Of   others to add   to your own,

Your growing powers.
 That you are   ready.

To whom is   your debt greater?
Cleave to the   second   woman.

JOHN

A flesh and blood woman, Tom,
Fanny is a reality;

And this but a letter.
This an abstraction.

TOM

Then you must confront
Temporarily

The flesh and blood author of the letter.
But a letter. Now compose your reply.

JOHN

Will she visit me here?
Why do I hesitate?

I've little stamina.
Is it weariness?

TOM

Hearing Perotin's motets
Do you forget what happened?

In Notre Dame with Marcel
Your energy redoubled,

Brought the threat of dire symptoms…
Even beyond your safety.

JOHN

But a revelation, Tom!
Yes! A unique experience!

The meaning of a line,
First,   familiarity.

The   meaning of a *second* line
Then, a wondrous double meaning.

Cemented   to the first:
Two lines heard as one line,

A   third,   *larger*   meaning –
And Tom! Three *true meanings,*

A   third!
The third

The threat was real,
The   creation

But I survive with larger purpose.
Of   ardent   imagination.
Fevers of poetry's eruption.

TOM

Then the game's a great one.
You make the   argument

Write to   her
Yourself. Write.

Joseph enters.

JOSEPH

I   thought   you   promised me
John seems flushed; it   could be

Recumbancy, you villain.
   Recovery......or   fever.

JOHN

There, an honest man again.
  Joseph forgives everything.

JOSEPH

You've thought about   the letter?
  Will   this   help or hinder him?

JOHN

I   have.
Yes, yes.

JOSEPH

Will you see her?
 It   goes farther.

JOHN

If she will see me.
Do I hope she will?

JOSEPH

Then   I remove objection.
  I would deny him nothing.

JOHN

Thank you, Joseph.
   I   am   relieved.

JOSEPH

Marcel speaks well of her.
I will   be   wholehearted.

She hadn't wished to see you
This   woman   is discreet.

Before this, fearing she'd disturb you.
* I can understand her   diffidence.*

She overcame her diffidence
Her fear was   reasonable.

Fearing that you'll leave for home, for England,
* I   can   understand   her changing her mind.*

Before she   had   a chance to make her case.
Missing you would be heartbreaking for her.

Besides, Marcel is   sure
Oh, yes, Marcel, of course,

A   female   friend will do you good.
Has his strange view   of what you need.

JOHN

A   female friend…well.
What a fine   fellow…

JOSEPH

Someone else to talk to, at least.
She will   encourage him, surely.

A person of appreciable substance.
She is certainly more learned than I.

JOHN

I'm   glad   to hear you grant
Your views are   enlarging

Such substance to a woman –
To   include   the other sex –

With   inflated   views of me.
Even when they're mistaken.

JOSEPH

Inflated   views, my modest friend?
How little you know of yourself.

Everything   she says is true.
Her judgment reveals wisdom.

JOHN

I   hope to   justify
Well, be that as it may,

Your confidence in me,
  An adventure awaits,

Joseph – and hers.
And we shall see…

The garret a week later.

JOHN

I'm   grateful to you for coming here,
Oh! How will I maintain composure?
I   …   will explode!

Mademoiselle Bonnot.
I must not frighten her.

VIVIENNE

I would need to possess
He is   as stirred as I.

Your poet's genius, Mister Keats,
   I   must put words together,

To   tell you of the honor I feel
Prove that I   am a   reasonable

To be   allowed to   sit   beside you.
Creature, not frighten him, reassure

If your habit were
Him of my, of my…

To hold your   court at the Pole,
Of my what? What do I   feel?

And you bade me come,
  I   am…yes…undone.

I'd go forthwith.
 I must be calm.

JOHN

I was ready   to apologize   all the more
I will be calm. Sentences are my stock in trade,

For your traversal of   the   city,
After all,   and I will not distress

But you assure me that
Her with   incoherence,

The Pole itself   is not too far,
  Even though I have never felt

So I rest content,   having
Less coherent – less controlled.

Spared you frozen seas and angry gales.
  A   metaphor: that will have to do.

VIVIENNE

There you are –
What to say?

My   coming the merest nothing.
Something conventional, stupid.

JOHN

Far from that.
Conventions.

Far from it.
They will pass.

Your kindness is a wonder.
  We are both   discomfited –

Your letter   has…
  But not for long.

VIVIENNE

Oh, Mister Keats,
  I can now speak,

It's I   who live in wonder of you.
Knowing the name of what I now feel.

Each time I read your Odes
   I   can describe my joy

My eyes and ears,
In your poetry,

The tips of my fingers,
Your effect on my heart,

My very heart
My very heart.

Are rendered open to wonder,
What was closed, opened. My senses

To all sensation, pain, and pleasure
Are intermingled with thoughts, and thoughts

As they had never before been open.
With color, texture, music, and movement:

I am on reading newly born.
I must stop; I must catch my breath.

JOHN

You say that honor
 Come to rest, Vivienne.

Is conferred on you
Time belongs to us.

That we speak here,
Would that I could

But what honor it is for me
Take your hands, press them, feel their warmth.

To think that poems of mine
But that will come, I know.

Affect you as I would hope they might.
There is a great deal to be said.

My life is justified –
We begin together.

To   be   for   another
Our lives are now one life.

What you say I have been for you.
  I   begin that life   justified.

VIVIENNE

Your life is more than justified.
  Can I speed his   recovery?

JOHN

I   must know more about you.
You heal   by   your being here.

VIVIENNE

More   about   me…
   I will speak, then.

I've long been struck by language.
Such   happy   years of   study…

I've asked myself repeatedly
Comparing many lexicons,

How words are   concatenated,
  Judging   this syntax and that one,

To select from secret thoughts,
In awe of the   mysteries

Against our will as well as with it,
Of private intention, utterance,

What will emerge into public worlds.
   Effects intended, not intended,

Some have said that everything we think
   Wondering whether everything thought

Can be so moved. I came to doubt this.
Can be said. Are there unspeakable

I took to languages so I might find the truth.
Rather than merely unspoken thoughts, emotions?

JOHN

An ancient question, Mademoiselle,
What was it Aristotle said?

Whether words record everything we think.
   If we can think something, we can speak it?

I'm no less absorbed with it.
Am I now in doubt of that?

I've believed what you doubt.
And if the Greeks were wrong?

Does not the poet transmute inner speech,
Have I looked too long to Attic thought?

Both formed and seeming-formless inner speech,
What you imply, Vivienne, changes the world.

Into what we hear and understand,
Ought I go on defending a view

And to which we can speak in turn?
That may be less ample than yours?

VIVIENNE

Could not some of inner speech
Who am I to question you,

Disguise those stirrings often felt
The greatest of all our poets?

To live apart from speech entirely?
But I must speak…and, I pray, help you.

JOHN

Perhaps. Yes, perhaps.
I am strongly moved.

My friends more versed in instrumental music
You want my life larger, calmer, happier;

Imply that words cannot reach
And you can bring that to me:

All depths of inner life,
I am certain of it.

Allowing Mozart access
Who better than Mozart to

To stirrings such as those you name.
Be your agent, my dear Vivienne?

VIVIENNE

My correspondent Thomas Young,
You understand me exactly.

Upon whose work the great Champollion has built,
I can show you the calm of silent Egypt,

Suggests to me,   implicitly,   that Mozart's great string quintets
The mirror of the counterpoint of Mozart's singing bowed strings.

Resemble hieroglyphs:
As one, so the   other,

They take us with them
Both burrowing down

To inner worlds   inaccessible
To   the hot alchemic cauldron

To   modern   speech and modern script.
Where things, tones, words melt   together.

JOHN

Your wish that I become
  I   will live in Paris

A   pupil of   Champollion…
And in ancient Egypt, at once.

I've thought of little else
The   magic of Egypt

Since your letter   came   to me.
And   the magic brought by you

I   will, dear Mademoiselle,
Are   irresistible.

Beg Champollion to take   me as his   student.
  I   crave study, to learn other minds and worlds,

And to please you further,
And to   feel   the   glory

I'll add pursuit of Mozart, beyond need of words,
Of pure music more deeply, so that   I might sing

To attendance   on Perotin's motets, replete with words.
As Mozart sings and polytextual motets fill   the   naves

I   remain   in Paris.
Of soaring cathedrals.

VIVIENNE

What joy you bring us!
  I   am faint with joy.

JOHN

I'd hoped for many months
To   begin   once   again,

That I might rest from   poetry,
Even   to   forget my past work,

And instead resume my education.
To   return to childhood's naivety

I   felt a   lack of true   readiness
And proceed slowly toward manhood.

To begin my   larger work.
I want a strong foundation

But at   the same time,
On which to build well.

I thought, In what does education
But what will count as a foundation?

Consist for me?
You reveal it.

Mademoiselle, to you I   owe my answer.
How   wonderful   a gift you've given me:

I've found my university.
My   future course of study.

VIVIENNE

I'll speak to Champollion in Grenoble.
I'll   gather   myself in   your service.

His   English lacks   no   subtlety;
What Champollion knows, you will know.

If he has not as yet
I cannot wait until

Devoured your work, he will.
I   hear   him speak of you.

He'll then insist on
 He will fasten on

Passing on to you
To your poetry

Everything he takes
As   only   he can.

From the   Rosetta   Stone.
Then I'll hasten straight to

I'll see Abbe Sicard tonight.
The other master of silence,

I'll be   indefatigable in your service.
Sicard. He will be entranced with your great project.

JOHN

You've renewed my strength.
 I'm   ready   to   start.

VIVIENNE

I'll   go   now.
Rest now, John.

My strength, too, renewed.
My strength, too, renewed.

The garret two weeks later.

JOHN

You tell me, Monsieur Champollion,
He listens   uncannily   closely.

That symbolism performs its functions
This   word, "symbol," has its secrets.

In ways more subtle…
You seem to know them.

CHAMPOLLION

…and   more different…
…more than subtlety…

JOHN

…more subtle and more different
…you   insist, and quite rightly.

Than I – or you? – before imagined.
The old   definitions   don't apply;

Is   poetry as it stands
Must poetry itself be

Then   compromised?
  Redefined?   How?

CHAMPOLLION

You wish assurance, Mister Keats.
This must worry a sincere poet.

I cannot give it.
But proper worry

Poetry is compromised.
May make truer poems.

JOHN

I'm alarmed to hear you say it.
I must learn what he means by that.

CHAMPOLLION

Perhaps I spoke incautiously.
I do not mean to alarm you.

It's better to say
I will rephrase this.

That poetry *was* compromised,
It's not a recent event;

Long ago, and so, alas, it remains.
We have inherited this compromise.

JOHN

Please explain, Monsieur.
Events in the past?

CHAMPOLLION

A choice was made, long ago,
It's a shadowed history,

Between two ways to see a symbol.
In which few have been interested.

What we came to call a symbol holds a place for something else,
You will do well to study the ways one thing stands for another;

One and only one other thing –
Much depends on how that happens.

A useful, mathematical notion,
We have been seduced by precision

The sense of symbol that builds a modern state.
And by the manipulation of matter.

Or, contrariwise, a symbol gathers meanings to itself,
Of far greater moment is the accumulation of meanings

Becoming ever thicker with thought and feeling –
That poetic symbolism gives us freely.

A noble, poetical notion, not useful, but noble.
Useful symbols must be the servants, poetry the master.

The poetical notion,
Then the world will be set right,

Eh, Mister Keats?
Don't you agree?

JOHN

Indeed.
Yes, yes.

CHAMPOLLION

Egyptian hieroglyphs
Surrender the future.

Are of the latter kind.
The past accumulates,

But words set down in *alphabetic* scripts,
The   present   prefers only to   substitute;

Today   the scripts of all   peoples save perhaps the Chinese,
Persons and   objects change, but they   remain light – in Europe.

Stand each for one thing   only…
 Lightness is   pathos, or worse.

JOHN

…for spoken words.
…to write, to speak…

CHAMPOLLION

Yes, for spoken words
Writing mimics speech,

Which themselves   refer
Not thought, which subsists

To single things alone.
In   interior   silence.

JOHN

And a written   hieroglyph
 I understand his direction

Is   to a spoken hieroglyph…
Save for an   ambiguity.

CHAMPOLLION

Hieroglyphs are never spoken.
 I must be   especially clear:

Because   they mean so much at once
They can have   many   referents,

They *can't* be   spoken.
And   we have one throat!

They're silent, to be sure,
 An   unusual silence

But   *this*   silence…fills.
That "says" more than speech.

JOHN

Mademoiselle Bonnot
 Just as she   implied:

Refers to plenitudes,
Full visual silences,

To silence, and the eye, not the ear.
  Testimony   to   simultaneity.

CHAMPOLLION

Yes. Rather than precision
There is a   dryness in one

And singularity…
Referent by itself.

JOHN

"Singularity,"   you say.
What is it about this word…

I beg your pardon.
But please continue.

CHAMPOLLION

Singularity,
As I was saying,

Speech, and the ear –
   Having one throat

Which, I add, together mark the time of clocks,
   Has decisive, if accidental effects,

As one spoken word after another
Giving sequences of single events

Ticks and ticks again, *ad infinitum.*
   Far too much prominence in our lives.

We enjoy plenitude.
The universe is filled;

And in plenitude, time stops.
   In that case, there is no time.

JOHN

In a plenum
In a plenum

There is no time…
There is no time…

CHAMPOLLION

Hieroglyphic writing
Does he understand yet?

Has no past or future tense.
   Insofar   as   hieroglyphs

The world in all its parts and   processes,
Multiply meanings, fill with their meanings,

In   all the fullness from which people
They fill the   universe: thus time stops.

In modern days take but a part,
The role of the   devout   poet

Is concentrated   in   the   present moment
Is no less than to stop time, defeating death.

And   it remains…in the present moment.
Keats will come to   understand this better

Single meanings give us   time and death.
In the course of learning   Egyptian.

Many meanings lift these curses from us.
He will overcome   alphabetic   words

Our choice is…
In   sequence.

JOHN

Precision or plenitude.
We either empty or fill.

CHAMPOLLION

Yes!
Hah!

JOHN

I hear these things you say,
Description   is   useful,

And say such things myself,
  Perhaps   necessary,

To myself, but hypocritically.
But it's not warm experience;

I've no experience of truly   what it is
It's not woven into my thoughts and senses

To which you refer.
  Consequentially.

CHAMPOLLION

Regard a circle, Mister Keats.

Draw a horizontal diameter:

It cuts the circle twice,

At eastern and western points.

Draw a vertical diameter:

It also cuts the circle twice,

At northern and southern points.

JOHN

Yes, Monsieur.
  I   see   it.

The circle is cut in quadrants.
It affects me in a strange way.

CHAMPOLLION

Splendid, splendid.
 Very good – yes.

What *are* these quarters

To readers of this hieroglyph?

They signify, at once,

The rooms, four, of the reader's house,

The regions, four, of his village,

And the quadrature of heaven,

All in harmony, each with the other two.

Now draw a hawk at the eastern point,

A mountain in the south,

A ram in the west,

A fire in the north…

JOHN

A   stunning picture…
I've seen this before…

CHAMPOLLION

…a *storied* picture:

The hawk at sunrise, birth;

The ram at sunset, death;

The mountain is endurance;

The fire dissolution.

To each direction

Adheres a hundred stories.

Why should one depart

From such a symbol

To another one?

Remain before it, rather.

One's mind and life then fill;

Time comes to a halt

In this plenum.

JOHN

A   single   hieroglyph?
One sign, many meanings!

CHAMPOLLION

Yes! One!
 He   sees!

JOHN

Each hieroglyph…each … a poem?
There is no call   for   syntax!

CHAMPOLLION

You understand what I have been saying.
Relationships   among signs don't matter.

JOHN

The voice supplanted silence – when?
A   historical   event,   then.

CHAMPOLLION

Twenty, perhaps thirty centuries ago.
Before   interest in history   begins.

JOHN

And since, you think?
So   long   ago…

CHAMPOLLION

Very little poetry,
Only diminution.

Quite against the world's   opinion.
Literary   judgment was fooled.

JOHN

Poetry, then, must overcome
Our   received   literary

An absence and a presence as well:
History   has been poorly written.

The absence   of a symbolism that gathers meaning –
We have not been aware of slow   accumulation,

Of hieroglyphic fullness,
   Accumulated meanings,

And the presence of a symbolism that merely substitutes –
Having become too used to unique combinations of words.

The alphabets and their often empty voices.
We have not thought well on the history of words.

CHAMPOLLION

A double overcoming.
You've absorbed the argument.

JOHN

Has Mademoiselle Bonnot
You've spoken with Vivienne:

Discussed Sicard with you?
The language of the deaf?

CHAMPOLLION

Yes. Enthralling work.
   A brilliant fellow.

JOHN

Your best opinion:
The relationship

Can silent gestures fully duplicate
Of our two means of symbolizing,

What hieroglyphs present us?
Hieroglyphs and signing hands?

CHAMPOLLION

I think they can.
By heaven, they're

No, I know it.
  Equivalent!

JOHN

Egyptian   can never be my language
This could not be more important to me,

Of   composition;
More remarkable,

The gestures of the deaf
Or   more   unexpected.

Can not be written down.
But what shall I do with

What shall I   do
What   I have learnt?

With what I know a poem might be?
  Perhaps I have not learnt enough?

Shall I see you next week, Monsieur?
  I   am resolved to   persevere.

CHAMPOLLION

With paints and brushes, Mister Keats.
 We   want   practice,   more practice,

We'll draw and color   hieroglyphs
More work with matter, much slow work.

With greater   permanence than this.
You will have   evidence   of all

It's thus you'll have experience
We've spoken of   until now.

Of   plenitude   through line and tint;
Your mind will work   differently

And since it's work of hands and eye,
While you draw and paint, and afterward,

Perhaps this other   work   of hands,
As you contemplate what you've done.

Sicard's   appropriation of the means
And then your other route to another

Our urchins of   the streets who cannot speak   employ to
Use of the mind, brought to you by the soundless children

Make themselves clear and more than clear
Who have solved their crippling problem

To   each other –
With true genius.

Perhaps   this   other work of hands
Both routes ask   for   repetition,

May disclose its role in future   poetry.
The   methodical   training of your hands.

Joseph's sitting room, London, 1825.

JOSEPH

Good news, I think.
 Will you think so?

134

JOHN

Certainly.
I'm not sure

I   suppose   so.
What I'm to think.

JOSEPH

Suppose?
Be sure.

JOHN

We were once engaged.
An   obligation.

JOSEPH

When young and stupid.
 No   one   is   exempt.

JOHN

Yes.
Hm.

JOSEPH

You want her happy.
Both are   better off.

JOHN

I   do.
Of course.

JOSEPH

Fanny   is   shallow, if vivacious.
No more than a   superficial girl,

"A minx," you said back then.
    Petulant   and   stubborn.

Durant   is shallow   too –
She found a perfect match –

A perfect   complement.
Good luck to both of them.

JOHN

At all events,
That is over.

Vivienne and I   are here.
Our new life has begun.

JOSEPH

The time at last:
England again!

The time of   restoration,   John.
What amazement you will bring us.

The strength of English epic
 Beyond Milton in both form

Recovered.
And substance.

Oh, the *time*;
I fear I've

I must run off.
Stayed much too long.

JOHN

My thanks for coming, Joseph.
You think you tire me, Joseph,

You represent my continuity –
And I can not shake your conviction.

London to Rome, Rome to Paris, Paris home.
Our travels first saved, then enlarged my life.

How true a friend you've been to me.
Can a friendship be more selfless?

JOSEPH

And you to me, and you to me.
You know how much you've done for me…

Joseph leaves.

JOHN

The time at last, he said.
For what am I ready?

TOM

You can now begin.
The moment is ripe.

JOHN

Can I in fact prepare to write?
What does it mean to be ready?

TOM

Of course you can.
Your education

You'll rise to   epic   that   reveals
Has prepared you for your new task,

The depths of human feeling
To   reveal   the foundation

Hitherto   concealed.
Of thought and feeling

And more: that draws from all
In such   a   way   as   to

Who hear and see your work
Strengthen the   foundation

Intensities. "Soul-making,"
And enlarge the structures

Do you remember?
  Erected   on it.

JOHN

The vale of soul-making…
Larger   than   inference.
The deep valley of mind.

TOM

Champollion proved to you
The heart of   Egypt, John.

That greater   depth of thought and feeling
The signs made in   Egypt and that made

Was known before to humankind,
   Egypt – how glorious a circle.

And can be known again.
We must reclaim that depth.

JOHN

Undeniable proof.
I'm utterly convinced.

TOM

Sicard proved to you
And this parallel

That certain gestures reproduce
   Revelation, that flying hands

The depths Egyptian hieroglyphs express.
Can fill the world and stop the course of time…

JOHN

And gesture can be seen…
Eyes following two hands…

TOM

On a stage, John,
To speak and sign

The stage on which your epic is performed.
   Before others, a bardic role to play.

JOHN

Performers of these epics…
I must train both performers

Will they sign and speak at once?
And my new   audience.

Can gestures fill the time that extended syllables provide them?
There will be   unprecedented techniques, a new pedagogy.

Can sounds and their meanings
 I   was   educated;

Borne by   spoken words and *heard*
 So must all   inhabitants

Join such gestures, *seen,*
 Of the new   theater,

And make my meanings larger?
The bard and   audience, be.

TOM

Why may not their signs
All   of us,   actors

Enthrall the eye while their words
And acted   upon,   will grow

Enthrall   the ear?
Through hands and voice –

A counterpoint of growing meanings.
 An   education   of   educations.

Later in the day.

VIVIENNE

A friend has come to see us, John.
 Wisdom   truly   inheres in cheer.

JOHN

Marcel! How good of you
We'll smile tonight, I think.

To make the journey.
 Depend   upon   it.

MARCEL

For   you and lovely Vivienne, anything.
Gad, they appear to   be happy as pups .

I said to myself, Marcel,
Paris is boring just now;

Betake your indolent   self across the Channel.
I'm sure to be received well   in jolly England.

How can Keats arrange affairs   without your help,
The truth is, I miss these young aspirants   to

Eh, Marcel, you dog?
The meaning of life.

VIVIENNE

Darling Marcel implored me
Could anyone   be more kind?

To tell   him   frankly   whether
Marcel would have returned home

Your work and spirits
  Before   disturbing

Were such that visiting us
John or   me in any way.

Would not tax you.
His manner may

As always, the heart of kindness
Be extravagant, but his soul

Behind the flaneur's mask.
Is pure benevolence.

MARCEL

Calumny. Pure, intended calumny.
I treasure my reputation, you know.

That you should entertain
Do not jeopardize it!

The smallest possibility
If my little ventures in the

That motives other than those
Protection of the helpless

Of self-regard can drive me,
Are discovered, I will not

Shocks me to the quick.
Hear the end of it.

JOHN

Do sit, old friend.
You will ever

Take wine with us
Conceal your heart,

And tell the news of Paris.
But your acts are eloquent.

MARCEL

Sicard may miss your company
Neither of your two professors

Even more than our friend Champollion does.
Has ever instructed the likes of you.

JOHN

I was merely their student.
They were kind to instruct me.

MARCEL

You were never "merely" anything, my boy.
You are serious; but really, that is a joke.

The poet John Keats one's student…
All peoples are your students.

JOHN

I confess to missing them,
What pleasure I took in my

Their wisdom and their forbearance.
Lessons, what illumination.

MARCEL

I'd walk with Sicard
I felt part of it.

To your and Severn's digs
On the perimeter,

Twice and more each week.
Even there, I could

We'd leave a wedge of silent children
Feel the heat and hear the strong music

Signing at your door.
Of your education.

He would often speak to me
  Sicard perceived all of that

Of your magnetic presence.
And kindly included me.

JOHN

To learn to sign from him is more than learning.
Hand-signing is very much more than it seems.

One's inner life acquires softness
You look at the face before you

And size and receptivity
With acutest concentration,

That seem to come by night, quite of themselves.
Your own face coming to conform with it,

Sicard's instruction may be of signs;
And somehow you inhabit that mind.

The consequence feels much like moral growth.
How like my "negative capability."

VIVIENNE

He talked to me in just those terms
  Sicard loved being in the same

About your person and poetry.
Room with you, talking and signing.

MARCEL

Each of you became
    Reciprocity,

The curriculum of the other.
Or I do not know its true meaning.

VIVIENNE

And Champollion?
How does he fare?

MARCEL

Learning tongues a mile a minute.
He is indefatigable!

I've never heard of most of them.
Who speaks all those strange languages?

Unlike Sicard, he owns a concrete record
Champollion's memories are readily

Of your weekly sessions –
    Available to him,

Shall I say, bespattered with paint.
 If in messy, colorful form.

JOHN

Half our hieroglyphic exercises!
We were like small children coloring

The other half is mine.
And we were like elders

I treasure it.
At the same time.

MARCEL

As you must.
A treasure.

JOHN

And so, Marcel, how long
Please tell us that you stay

Will you remain in England?
With us indefinitely.

MARCEL

Some weeks, in self-duress, I think.
Alas, I belong in Paris.

I plan to stroll among your cities
I will find some amusement, I think,

Recording my impressions.
Wandering about a while,

I expect considerable interest
And I won't make the mistake of imposing

In the memoirs I plan to write –
On such good friends as you've become.

When I get around to it.
I was not born yesterday.

VIVIENNE

You'll visit us often.
I'll hate to see you go.

MARCEL

When in London,
  I   begin to

I   glue myself to you.
Miss you both already.

You'll beg me to   depart.
* What   an odd world this is.*

JOHN

Never,   Marcel.
Stay on, my friend.

MARCEL

Then to prove your youthful constancy,
  I must stop this   philosophizing

Have supper   with me tonight
* And get back down to planning*

At   my redoubt   in   Piccadilly   Circus.
Some joyous occasions for the three of us.

VIVIENNE

Of course we will…John?
What fun   it   will   be.

JOHN

We descend on you at nine.
We can't see you too often.

MARCEL

Then good day 'til nine.
  I'll   outdo   myself.

Marcel leaves.

VIVIENNE

Now perhaps you'll sleep 'til...
  It has been a   tiring...

JOHN

No, Vivienne.
No, my dear.

I'm aswarm with thoughts
My mind is   racing,

Of   you in England now, away from Paris;
From your new   situation   here in London

Of my returning home so changed;
To my resumption of life here,

Of epic built   on   new assumptions
To a project fraught with   mystery,

Of what a signing speaker can achieve
Calling for yet unclear   conceptions

And what an audience, once prepared, can accept...
  Of relations   among   words, silence, music...

VIVIENNE

Do set your mind at ease
My   relation   to you,

With regard to me, at least.
  At least, is perfectly clear;

You know what life with you
  Surely   you   understand

Has become for me.
  This as well as I:

I feel surplus of life
I live in your radiance.

Each day because
You are sun to

You lie   beside   me.
  Me, my warmth and light.

JOHN

Your home in Paris, Vivienne…
  I've taken you away from…

VIVIENNE

You're my home.
  Enough, John.

So to your writing, John, your writing.
We no longer need   to   talk about

What will be your subject?
Each   other. We are safe.

JOHN

Ah, yes, my subject…
  I have an idea

My thoughts have come this far:
Drawn from the   inscriptions –

Among the drawings on Egypt's   funerary walls
   Unforgettable   inscriptions – we hovered over.

Shown to me   by   Champollion,
Champollion stopped there himself.

I came upon   a slim woman,
I could not proceed beyond her.

A votary   of Isis,   Champollion surmised.
Whatever a goddess is,   she is one   surely –

She plays two end-blown flutes at once.
* The goddess playing   her   music.*
* I heard her! I heard   her   music!*

VIVIENNE

How   is that accomplished?
Two flutes at the same time?

JOHN

The ends brought to her lips,
   Anatomy's   limits

Are close beside each other.
Are brilliantly ignored.

The farther ends are widely spaced
She has but the one throat all have,

To grant each hand its freedom   on each flute.
But one   passage   of air – now becomes two,

One hand plays a   tune, the other plays another.
   Permitting two different melodies their exits.

And think: the triangular shape
Can this   symbolism   be

Made by the double-flute when played
   Coincidental?   Impossible!

Is the symbol of woman, Vivienne!
One melody is male, two female.

Double song, the feminine, and ancient   Egypt…
    Generation: we are given more than we had.
                     Most ancient of hopes.

VIVIENNE

My breath is coming quickly. Go on.
Such   exalted   correspondences!

JOHN

I   cannot help but think
The motets of Notre Dame…

That she   achieves what I aspire to do.
They were not simply a novel technique

My two melodies made of words,
In a   narrow tradition of

A melody   spoken,   a melody signed,
Musical art; they were   specifically

Create between them – between the two   of them,
Written to   induce   a state of mind valued

A third melody,
Above all others.

But one not made of words.
Do I not wish to do

Is it made of silent feelings?
A similar thing myself,

Might these feelings, if only now and then,
Defining the state of mind differently,

Be new to us, not attached to words
And valuing it more highly than

Because never known before?
Christians value states of grace?

Thus our store of feeling grows!
That state of mind requires an

I seek the third melody, Vivienne.
Adequate definition of mind

I dream about this woman who serves Isis,
Itself, just as the cure of an illness

About her silent added melody – and mine.
Requires a diagnosis that implies the cure.

VIVIENNE

She has come to life.
You know this woman.

JOHN

I begin to know myself
Could mind be a palimpsest?

As bound by our particulars
Are there layers of the mind

To   a   shallow comprehension
Such that the thin   surface layer

Of the   depth of   woman's mind
Contains our male   instruments –

And the mystery   of   music.
Precision, order, and the rest –

My   slowly growing, if faltering   understanding
Where the next, deeper layer, the female, alters them,

Of your heart, Vivienne, and
Adding   soft   metaphor,

My dreams about   the wondrous flautist
Transforming prose into   what we know

Have relieved me of my youthful musings
As   poetry? And of deeper layers still?

On Attic myths and   Celtic   tales,
A   third layer, of the night's dreams,

Both but realms of boys grown old.
Told by   older   languages;

I must wander in   the oldest streets
Finally, perhaps,   a fourth layer,

Of   ancient Egypt,   the realm of such as Isis,
The foundation, where distinctions disappear,

Listening   for their music.
And the deepest music plays.

VIVIENNE

Begin   now, John.
Sing all of   mind.

JOHN

Yes. I will.
Tom and I.

An elaboration of "Keats at Thirty," in Marvin Bram, *Negative Capability* (2012).

The Mastersingers

Whale

              gravamen
              contemplate   sharp
Crystalline, milky white   There, cliffs
              porcelain   steep
              ruminate

                  fired
                  tiered
Angled, faceted, joined
                  spired
                  reared

          height   peak
Look: that bird, the sun, that seal, the snow
                            dark   sleek

We leap, we dive, we never go

Very far.

Sloth

The sloth made no sound the forest animals could hear.

Think? I never stop! All my thoughts pile up
Thank you, but no; I'd   rather   not   look down

And make a place among our sounds and sights.
Where the ground animals   live. Noisy   lives,

Polysemy

Nothing   else happens. Thought, sound, color, movements
Where too much happens,   where   too   much surprises,

Of   my fur fill my life. My branch
And there is no time to   ponder.

My home. Sidwise movement to my fruit,
I   look   upward   only,   at the sky

Among   white   flowers.
Through my tree's branches.

Winds blow along my   body – rippling,   braiding   patches
Birds   fly   across the daytime sky, among shimmering leaves;

Of fur. Breezes restore me,   fill corners, light
The stars rise and turn in black, brilliant   night.
Tree-trunk time is strong, downward winding time.

Horizons   in my landscape thoughts.
No surprises; and freedom   to think,
Our moments are detached,   complete.

I go nowhere, desire nothing,   and expect
To   imagine everything – all sounds and colors,
We are given all the time, all the fruit and flowers,

My happiness   to grow   season
All sensations;   the fullest   music,
The summer winds, the fullness of thought,

After   green season.
Silent   and my own.
The dark forest's song.

Earthworm

I'm not supposed to have　　intentions,
People　set　their watches by Kant's walks.

Being　too primitive – "basic" is the word I prefer –
He had the most ambitious　plan　imaginable,

So you'll likely think of this as
To　tell　us with such precision

Anthropomorphic , or "lumbricomorphic" –
That he felt that he had to invent words to

My　being an　earthworm – I suppose.
Meet his standard, what　　reality

But　attempt agnosticism on the question of intentions.
Is　and what reality　definitively,　　　unarguably

What do　any　of　us know of others,
　Is　not. He appeared largely　satisfied

Men – I mean by that all human beings – of worms,
That　he　had completed his enormous　　project.

Worms of　men; men of men, worms of worms?
　You　see, what　we believe　is　　surely,

Polysemy

So I'll be declarative about intentions:
Unquestionably real is in fact the alloy

I *intend* to chew up earth and leave behind
Of what is   real-but-unapproachable,

The tunnels that receive   the air and water
In   effect, "behind" what we believe is real,

In   the absence of which plants would not grow
And the contingent,   human   –   as   distinct

And animals would not appear on earth.
From turtle or mayfly – central nervous

Be   respectful of us worms, you vainglorious animals.
System. The worm, for   example,   co-creates and occupies

You owe us very much more than you think.
 A   universe very different   from ours.

Men and worms cross universes,
For each   central nervous system,
Crossing   universes   create

Benevolently   only   in one direction.
A separate, distinctive universe exists.
Contrapuntal temporalities, silent music.

Made in the USA
San Bernardino, CA
10 May 2016